Exactly as You Are

EXACTLY AS YOU ARE

The Life and Faith of Mister Rogers

Shea Tuttle

WILLIAM B. EERDMANS PUBLISHING COMPANY
GRAND RAPIDS, MICHIGAN

Wm. B. Eerdmans Publishing Co.
4035 Park East Court SE, Grand Rapids, Michigan 49546
www.eerdmans.com

25 24 23 22 21 20 19   1 2 3 4 5 6 7

ISBN 978-0-8028-7655-3

Library of Congress Cataloging-in-Publication Data

Names: Tuttle, Shea, 1983– author.
Title: Exactly as you are : the life and faith of Mister Rogers / Shea Tuttle.
Description: Grand Rapids, Michigan : William B. Eerdmans Publishing
    Company, 2019. | Includes bibliographical references. |
    Summary: "Exactly as You Are: The Life and Faith of Mister Rogers
    pursues a rich understanding of this good, kind, sometimes strange,
    deeply influential, holy man: the neighborhood he came from, the
    neighborhood he built, and the kind of neighbor he, by his example,
    calls all of us to be even now, in our own troubled time"—Provided
    by publisher.
Identifiers: LCCN 2019022638 | ISBN 9780802876553 (hardcover)
Subjects: LCSH: Rogers, Fred—Religion. | Television personalities
    —United States—Biography. | Presbyterian Church—United
    States—Clergy—Biography. | Mister Rogers' neighborhood
    (Television program) | Television and children. | Moral education.
Classification: LCC PN1992.4.R56 T88 2019 | DDC 791.4502/8092 [B]—dc23
    LC record available at https://lccn.loc.gov/2019022638

For Kyrianne and Halley,
and for Drew

CONTENTS

BROADCASTING GRACE

Mr. Rogers' Neighborhood

Contents

HELLO, NEIGHBOR

Finding Fred Rogers

ACKNOWLEDGMENTS

I t is more clear to me than ever that writing a book is the work of a neighborhood. Here are some of the friends and neighbors to whom I owe great thanks:

It was a joy to talk to people who knew Fred Rogers, including Randee Humphrey, Tom Junod, Cindy Kernick, Tim Madigan, John McCall, and Christopher de Vinck. Michael Horton and François Clemmons were particularly generous with their time and insights, and I'm grateful to know them both. I am also particularly grateful to Lisa Hamilton for trusting me with her remembrances. Thanks to Lynn Japinga for getting me in touch with Lisa. Lynn Johnson shared her memories and her photographs, which capture Fred's spirit like no others I've seen. I'm honored that she agreed to license one of her photos for the cover of this book.

Thanks to all at Fred Rogers Productions, especially Lynn Butler, who sent books and CDs, and Matthew Shiels, who worked with me on permissions. In addition to offering his own insights, Bill Isler enabled many connections and conversations that furthered this project. I'm grateful, too, to the team at the Fred Rogers Center at St. Vincent College, and especially to Emily Uhrin at the Fred Rogers Archive, who answered dozens of questions, pulled scores of documents, and knows so much more than I could ever think to ask about Fred and his life and work. Jim Okonak at the McFeely-Rogers Foundation was unfailingly kind, generous, and helpful.

I am greatly indebted to Tim Lybarger and the Neighborhood Archive at www.neighborhoodarchive.com. I cannot overstate the value of the site for referencing songs, episodes, characters, history, and more from *Mister Rogers' Neighborhood*, *The Children's Corner*, and beyond.

Fred's own neighborhoods were every bit as welcoming as one might hope. Debbie Herwick of Latrobe United Methodist Church, Arlene Jones and Rev. Clark Kerr of Latrobe Presbyterian Church, and Pamela Ferrero of the Latrobe Area Historical Society helpfully answered my questions. Rev. Carolyn Cranston, Dr. Helen Blier, and Anne Malone at Pittsburgh Theological Seminary also helped me check facts and satisfy curiosities.

I am grateful to Linda Meise, Anna Byrne, and Patricia Abrames for permitting me to quote their letters to Mister Rogers. Thanks as well to Joanna Milano and Mike Abrames for helping me get in touch with them. Thanks to Larry Nudelman for sharing his documents and stories.

Thanks to Jason Marsh, Jeremy Adam Smith, Kira Newman, Hong Nguyen, and *Greater Good Magazine* for the opportunity to write about Fred. Some of the material in chapter 12 appeared first in their journal. Thanks to Kristen Manieri at *The Synced Life Podcast* for great questions and conversation about Fred.

I am grateful to the whole team at Eerdmans and its members, past and present: Lil Copan, who guided me through the proposal process and delivered me to Eerdmans; David Bratt, whose insights were always pitch-perfect; freelance editor Victoria Jones, whose edits, fact-checks, and keen observations made this book infinitely better; and Linda Bieze, who shepherded the project through its final stages. Rachel Brewer has been a thoughtful and savvy conversation partner. Meg Schmidt designed the cover and conceived and drew the interior illustrations, and I couldn't be happier with them. Thanks to Leah Luyk for the lovely interior, Laura Bardolph Hubers for publicity work, and freelancer Tim Baker for proofreading. Additional thanks to Tracy Danz and Anita Eerdmans for early conversations, enthusiasms, and connections.

Christy Edwall, Megan Hunt Fryling, Chuck Mathewes, Kim Wagner, and Kristin Tuttle helped with Greek and French. Caroline Kelly, Elizabeth Stewart, and Nancy Myer clarified Presbyterian procedure. Thanks to all of them.

Thanks to the team at Spalding University's School of Creative and Professional Writing, especially Karen Mann and Kathleen Driskell. Spalding's program is flexible and compassionate enough to allow me to be on leave while working on this book, and it's been a gift to feel supported from a distance and to know that I can return at the right time to a welcoming writing home.

Thanks to Charles Marsh at the Project on Lived Theology for getting the conversation started and for writerly advice along the way. And thanks to Jessica Seibert for being such a good friend and collaborator at the Project. I'm grateful to Karen Wright Marsh for support, enthusiasm, and a couple of late-night chats in Grand Rapids. Thanks also to Peter Slade, who read an early draft of a short piece on Fred Rogers and helpfully reminded me of Fred's delightful strangeness.

Michael G. Long, the author of *Peaceful Neighbor: Discovering the Countercultural Mister Rogers* (among many other books), has been integral to this process. Mike's research was immensely helpful to me, and his collegiality, advice, kindness, and confidence have been generous beyond measure.

Meredith McNabb lent me a book for a very extended period and graciously cheered me on at every opportunity. Amanda Baier-Miles is a patient and brilliant photographer and a generous friend. I'm grateful for her compassion, support, and thoughtfulness. Josey Bridges Snyder helped with Hebrew and shared in kitchen table writing camp, and her friendship never falters across the miles or months (or years). I am thankful for and to Jack Ridl, who is a light in the world, and whose confidence in this project sustained me through more than a few seasons of doubt.

Aubrey Collins, Cheryl Klein, Hannah Shanks, Debbie Weingarten, and Jennifer Young, fabulous writers all, I'm so grateful for you I can hardly stand it. I couldn't possibly list all the ways you've helped this book happen, much less the countless strange and wonderful ways you've graced my life. Thank you.

Thanks to my mom, Angela Tuttle, my first and most dedicated reader, and to my dad, Rick Tuttle. Your steadfast support makes pretty much everything that's possible, possible. Thanks to Erin Lockridge and Kristin Tuttle for your endurance, excitement, and ideas, for tolerating my absences at Christmas, and for watching *Mister Rogers' Neighborhood* with me when we were little. Thanks to Brooke and Vicki Willson for caring for our kids so I could have writing camp(s!), and for your ongoing support.

Thanks to Drew for gifts too numerous to name: for being a smart critic, a staunch defender, a brilliant conversation partner, a theological co-creator, and my best friend.

Kyrianne and Halley, thanks for watching Mister Rogers with me, and for loving him, and for loving me, and for being you. I love you.

INTRODUCTION

Why hi, don't I know you?

Weekday afternoons when I was a child often found me curled up on the brown, plaid couch in our basement family room, draped in a homely, single-yarn brown afghan, my fingers poking through its open knit. I'd settle in as the opening sequence unfolded: the aerial view of the neighborhood giving way to a zoom shot of the house's exterior, the camera then cutting inside to the living room and panning toward the front door, through which a slender man entered with purpose, met my eyes for the first time, and smiled. The ascending piano chords, then the song, familiar as a prayer: "It's a beautiful day in this neighborhood, a beautiful day for a neighbor. Would you be mine?"

As he sang, he hung his blazer in the closet and put on a zippered sweater, then sat down and swapped his loafers for a pair of navy canvas sneakers by the time the song ended.

"Hello, neighbor," he'd greet me.

"Hello, Mister Rogers," I'd reply.

1

On many of our visits, he'd bring something with him—maybe pretzels, wooden blocks, or a musical instrument. He'd tell me a little bit about whatever it was before getting interrupted by a knock at the door or a phone call, which would often bring an invitation that would take us out into the neighborhood to visit the bakery or the music store, a restaurant or an arts center. Later in the program, once we had returned to the house, Mister Rogers would say, "Let's have some make-believe," and remind me of what was transpiring when last we visited the Neighborhood of Make-Believe, where a motley crew of people and puppets made their way through neighborhood politics, personal insecurities, and more.

Mister Rogers would summon Trolley, the cheerful red streetcar who guided the transition into Make-Believe, and I, from my corner of the couch, would let out a sigh—I preferred the segments of the show in Mister Rogers's company to the interlude in Make-Believe—but only a small sigh, because I knew that, in just a few minutes, Trolley would faithfully return me to that living room and to Mister Rogers. Then we would sing a little and talk about what we did that day and what we would do tomorrow. We'd acknowledge the wonderful ways I was growing, the good feelings that gave me, and my astonishing singularity in the world. And then we would say goodbye, until tomorrow.

Over the years, I grew out of *Mister Rogers' Neighborhood*. I forgot the storylines and many of the songs. But I remembered the man, and I remembered how he and his program made me feel: completely seen, completely loved. I cannot recall the precise origin of my affection for Mister Rogers, and I cannot quite explain its intensity. I just know that he is indescribably special to me; I feel as if I have always known him, like he was a part of my becoming. It is not simple nostalgia, fleeting and saccharine. It is deeper than nostalgia. It is formation. It is love.

There's a whole lot to say about Fred Rogers, who was a man of complexity—even contradiction. He was whimsical yet disciplined, a gentle control freak, deeply passionate yet measured, strange and beloved. He was, in the words of his friend Tom Junod, "a slip of a man"—5'11" and 143 pounds—yet had a will of iron.[1] He was, in ways, transparent: for many years, his wife, Joanne, has said of him, "What you see is what you get,"[2] and the TV writer James Kaplan once wrote that Fred Rogers in person was "more Mister Rogers than Mister Rogers."[3] But he was also, in ways, opaque. In 1989, John Sedgwick titled his *Wigwag* magazine profile of Fred "Who the Devil Is Fred Rogers?," and when those who knew him best set out to establish the Fred Rogers Center after his death in 2003, they asked each other, "OK, so who the hell was Fred?"[4] In the documentary *Won't You Be My Neighbor?*, Fred's own son says, "I sometimes wonder myself how he ticked."[5] Even Fred's self-definition is complex. Asked in 1986 who the real Mister Rogers was, he replied, as ever, slowly, thoughtfully: "I'm a composer and a piano player, a writer and a television producer . . . almost by accident, a performer . . . a husband and a father. And I am a minister."[6]

A minister. This role was essential to Fred's complex identity, though he didn't often foreground it publicly. Faith was a major part of who he was, and it had been from the very beginning. During his childhood, he spent virtually every Sunday morning in church. He planned to go to seminary following college but ended up changing course to work in television. In 1954, while working on his first children's program, he finally enrolled at Western Theological Seminary in Pittsburgh and began taking courses during his lunch hour. He was ordained a Presbyterian minister in 1963 and given a special charge to minister to children and families through the mass media. Within five years of his ordination, *Mister Rogers' Neighborhood* was airing nationwide. "It's very theological, what we do," Fred said about the program.[7]

In truth, Fred could have said that about pretty much any aspect of his life. He was a religious person through and through, extraordinarily thoughtful and intentional, and his faith was constantly present to him. He began every day at 5 a.m. with prayer and Bible study, talked frequently with close friends about matters of faith, and prayed each time he stepped onto the *Mister Rogers' Neighborhood* set, "Let some word that is heard be thine."[8]

When Fred looked into the lens of the camera and spoke to his "television neighbors," he offered his most core beliefs without ever speaking of God directly. "I'm giving the children myself and whoever I am," he said in 1974.

> Anything that's a part of me becomes a part of the program. My relationship with God, which I feel is very comfortable and healthy, cannot ever be disassociated from who I am on the program, even though I don't deal in overt theological terms. Our dialog with children constantly includes acceptance of someone exactly as she or he is at the moment. I feel that's how God operates. Jesus tells us in no uncertain terms that "I like you as you are and let's grow together from there."[9]

Without using the overt language of faith on the air, Mister Rogers relentlessly preached his gospel: you are loved just the way you are. He testified to this love with conviction despite knowing well that not all children live in a loving home (and he heard from many such children, over the years, who thanked him for representing a reality beyond their nightmarish households). He could preach love—and do it with such contagious conviction—because the message was rooted in something deeper than mere affection or transitory admiration: Fred's own belief in "a loving mystery at the heart of the universe that yearns to be expressed."[10] Fred worked hard every day to help express that loving mystery, to offer God's abundant love without condition to children, parents, *Neighborhood* staff, strangers on the street, people who wrote him letters—anyone and everyone who encountered him whether on television or in person. He did not do it perfectly—he was as human as you or me—but he did it extraordinarily.

"You know, when I decided to look for work in television, I couldn't possibly have known how I would be used," Fred said in 1994. "I've simply tried to be open to the possibilities God has made available to me."[11]

BECOMING
MISTER ROGERS

From Latrobe, Pennsylvania, to *Mister Rogers' Neighborhood*

1

CHILDHOOD, LOVE, AND FEAR

Are you brave and don't know it?

Fred McFeely Rogers was born on March 20, 1928, to Nancy McFeely Rogers and James Hillis Rogers, a wealthy couple living in the industrial town of Latrobe, Pennsylvania. Throughout his childhood, Fred was frequently ill, often missing school—sometimes for long stretches. When he was five years old, he spent an entire summer at his family doctor's house, which had the only air conditioner in town. (The AC unit was a joint purchase by the doctor, who had an asthmatic son, and the Rogers family. The two sick boys shared the single air-conditioned room all during ragweed season.)[1]

Around the time Fred was eight years old, he dreaded going to school. An only child until his sister was adopted when he was eleven, Fred was shy, more comfortable spending time with adults than with children. He missed school frequently because of his illnesses, and he was overweight. He became the target of school bullies.

Most days, the family's chauffeur drove Fred the few blocks to and from the Second Ward School, but one afternoon, his teacher dismissed the class early, and Fred decided to walk home.[2] It was not a short walk for a small boy, but it was also not an impossible one: a few blocks, all streets he knew well. He set off first past First Presbyterian Church, where he attended services with his family every Sunday, and then passed Latrobe Methodist Episcopal Church. He looked carefully before crossing Main Street, an artery to the downtown and the busiest street on his route, and then set off down Ridge toward Weldon, the street where he lived.[3]

Not long after he started walking, between the sounds of passing cars, he heard them—their footfall, a laugh with an edge, and then their voices: "Hey! Fat Freddy! We're going to get you!"

He felt the familiar flush of shame, hot in his belly, creeping up his neck, and his heart began to pound. He heard his parents' and grandparents' voices in his mind, speaking their usual counsel: "Just let on that you don't care," they urged him. "Then nobody will bother you." But he did care. He cared very much. And now the boys were getting closer. He willed his legs to go faster, his corduroy pantlegs zip-zipping against each other as he urged his jog toward a run.[4]

Freddy turned onto Weldon, but he still had three blocks to go—up an incline—before reaching home. With a wave of relief, he remembered that a kind widow, a friend of the family, lived along his route. He prayed that she would be home as he turned up her front walk and climbed her stairs. When Mrs. Stewart answered the frantic knock at her door, she found a flushed, panting boy, his face shining with exertion and fear. She let him in immediately. The bullies gave up and took off, looking for new entertainment, as bullies do, and Mrs. Stewart called Fred's house so someone could come and pick him up.

But Fred thought about those bullies for the rest of his life. "I resented the teasing. I resented the pain. I resented those kids for not seeing beyond my fatness or my shyness," he told audiences sixty years later, marveling at how well he still remembered that day. "And what's more," he said, "I didn't know it was alright to feel any of those things."[5]

Freddy—young, wise Freddy—took on the work of sadness on his own. He cried when he was alone—about the bullies, about his loneliness, about people's inability to see beyond the outside. He sat at the piano in his home and let his fingers find melodies to express his feelings. He talked to his puppets, and they talked to him. He started to look around him for other people who were struggling, other people who were sad, and he began to see that this included just about everybody—even the bullies themselves.

"I started to look behind the things that people did and said," the grown-up Fred Rogers said, looking back, "and, after a lot of sadness, I began a lifelong search for what is essential, what it is about my neighbor that doesn't meet the eye."[6]

———————

At home, Fred was safe and secure. His parents doted on him. Nancy was tender with her son, teaching him the lesson that floods social media following every national tragedy: "Look for the helpers. You will always find people who are helping." His father, Jim, one of the town's chief industrialists, was a compassionate boss, engaged with his employees and their lives, families, and needs. And though he was a busy man, often consumed by obligations beyond his home, he also found ways to nurture Fred. "There's an old family story which one of my parents' friends used to tell me," Fred remembered.

She'd say, "You know, Freddy, you were a colicky baby, and you cried a lot. And it was hard to get you to sleep; but, when your father would get home from work, he'd take you in his arms and go to the rocking chair and in a matter of minutes you'd be sound asleep—and *he* would be, too."[7]

When Fred was six, his grandfather Rogers, Jim's father, died. During the visitation, when his grandfather was lying in state, Fred found his father on the second floor of the house, crying.[8] His parents were not typically demonstrative with their so-called negative emotions, so this caught Freddy by surprise. He knew then that men could express deep feelings. Men—even his strong, powerful father who commanded every room he entered—could cry.

Fred's grandfather McFeely, Nancy's father, was another important figure in Fred's childhood—significant enough to be the namesake of the deliveryman in *Mister Rogers' Neighborhood*, Mister McFeely. He was the person who told young Freddy, "You've made this day a special day for me."[9] Grandfather McFeely, whom Fred called Ding Dong after a favorite nursery rhyme they shared, also encouraged the overprotected boy to take a few risks. Once, when Fred's family was visiting Ding Dong's farm, Fred climbed up on the old stone walls that zigzagged across the fields. His parents cautioned him and began to ask him to climb back down, but his grandfather interrupted: "Let the kid walk on the wall. He's got to learn to do things for himself."[10] Freddy felt empowered that day, and he always remembered how permission to take a risk was a special kind of love.

———

A sickly, often lonely boy who got teased by his classmates and struggled with his own body could have grown up into inhibition, bitterness, or bullying. Instead, he grew up into Mister Rogers, a man who looked into the camera every day and offered love, affirmation, and security to millions of scared kids in households across the nation. This was, in part, because his childhood was not most defined by those bullies; it was most defined by love: the love of his parents and grandparents first and foremost, as well as the love he received from his church and neighborhood community—a community we'll visit in the next chapter.

But another reason the bullied boy grew into the gracious Mister Rogers is that he didn't forget what it was like to be "Fat Freddy." Margaret McFarland, a renowned child psychologist and Fred's teacher, consultant, and friend, attributed Fred's unique insight into children to his ability to stay connected to his own childhood.[11] Fred knew intimately the current of fear mixed with elation that runs through so much of childhood, the electricity of the outside world that makes the return home so very sweet. And so he worked hard, every day of his television career, every time he looked directly into the camera's lens, to offer something of that home to the children who watched. In the space between his gaze and the gaze of each child watching, he created an intimate world of safety and calm.

Still, being a safe adult for children, in Fred's view, didn't mean he would deal only in benign topics. His critics missed this about him; when Mister Rogers was mocked and parodied, it was usually to suggest that he embodied life as it never really is: sanitized, sanded-off, falsely sweet and simple. But Mister Rogers spoke to children constantly of their fears. In the Neighborhood of Make-Believe, the playground of Fred's own imagination, weekly storylines often reckoned, in meaningfully complex ways, with the fears of children and adults. Daniel Striped Tiger in particular seemed to be afraid of nearly everything. *Mister Rogers' Neighborhood*'s very first week of national programming was built around the fear of change (though in this case, it's King Friday XIII who fears it most, going so far as to employ a border guard to interrogate all visitors for fear they will bring more change to the neighborhood—but more on this later).

When Fred acknowledged children's very real feelings and walked through those feelings with them, he was taking a cue from Christianity's central story: in the Gospels, God takes on humanness and enters the world in the person of Jesus; God participates, very personally, in human struggles and fear. Fred modeled this divine care intentionally. "When I say what we do [through *Mister Rogers' Neighborhood*] is theological, I'm referring to the Incarnation," he told an interviewer in 1971. "The Incarnation means man is not isolated. There is Someone who cares and understands."[12]

Mister Rogers's responses to his viewers' fears were patient, serious, and thorough. He didn't ask kids to stop being afraid—though sometimes his careful explanations *did* alleviate fear—or to stop crying. (It angered Fred to hear adults tell children not to cry, even when those adults were trying to offer comfort.[13]) Instead, he offered a kind of incarnation through his own loving presence. Through his memory of childhood, through the gentleness with which he held his own childhood feelings, Mister Rogers provided a comfort much greater than "Don't cry," "Don't be afraid," or even "Just let on that you don't care." God cared, Fred believed, enough to be among us and to feel every human feeling, and so Fred worked hard to be with children in their feelings, to explain and alleviate when possible, but more importantly, to take seriously—as seriously as God becoming human.

2

THE FIRST NEIGHBORHOOD

It's a beautiful day in the neighborhood.

Jim Rogers was a machinist at the McFeely Brick Company when he met Nancy McFeely, the owner's daughter. Thanks to Nancy's wealth, the couple had a good deal of money from the time they got married, and right away, they set about using it well. Jim convinced Nancy to buy Latrobe Die Casting Company, and eventually, they also owned Fullman Manufacturing and the McFeely Brick Company. Over time, Jim became one of the town's chief industrialists, and the family became one of the wealthiest in town.

Jim's office sat six stories high on the top floor of the tallest building in Latrobe, and from there, he made decisions about his factories and met with other leaders—the owners of the steel mills, plastic molds manufacturer, beer company, and more—when something went wrong in town. His employees came to see him there if they had a problem at home, and he would listen and help in any way he could. When he wanted to visit one of his factories, he would take off his coat and tie, roll up his sleeves, and put a plug of tobacco in his mouth. When he got to the floor, he knew all his employees—at one time, he had over five hundred of them—by name.[1]

While Jim was ministering to the factory workers' families and, through them, to the town more broadly, Nancy was carrying out her own service work. Each Christmas, her gift list included hundreds of names.[2] She bought a tie each year for every doctor in Latrobe,[3] and she knit a sweater each month for someone on her Christmas list. (When Fred grew up, he was a yearly recipient, and Nancy would be sure to make his a zippered cardigan so he could wear it on the *Neighborhood*.[4]) She also regularly cooked meals for those in need. "My mother was the original 'Meals on Wheels' person," Fred remembered. "Whenever she heard of someone who was sick or hungry, she'd show up wherever they were with a covered dish."[5] She spent time at the hospital on a regular basis, rocking babies in the nursery.[6] And when children or families were in need, the nurse at the elementary school would order shoes, coats, eyeglasses, or even furniture and have the bills sent directly to Nancy Rogers.[7]

Jim and Nancy took Fred and Laney, Fred's younger sister, to Latrobe Presbyterian Church each Sunday. They attended Sunday school and worship services there, and both parents served on church boards. Late in his life, Fred remembered his father once saying that "the church should always be a little bit in the red."[8] Though Jim was a man of finance, he believed that churches should be in the business of helping those who need it, not merely saving for an imagined rainy day.

Nancy and Jim loved Latrobe and felt it had been very good to their family. They wanted to find a more sustained way to continue investing in the community, so they established the McFeely-Rogers Foundation in 1953. Initially, the grantmaking was lean, amounting to about $250 per year, but over time, the foundation grew in wealth and influence.

Not long after the foundation was established, tragedy struck Latrobe. At the time, the parks department made use of a broad section of Loyalhanna Creek called Paddy's Hole to serve as a swimming area for residents. It was a popular place, especially for teenagers, and the department installed lifeguards who perched atop phone poles to monitor swimmers. But after a flash flood one summer, the water was high and cloudy, and a teenage boy from the neighboring town drowned. Nancy Rogers—along with the rest of Latrobe—was shocked and saddened. "Latrobe is better than that," she said, and the McFeely-Rogers Foundation began seeking partnerships with other local funding sources in order to provide Latrobe families with a safe place to swim. They built a town pool, now called the Rogers-McFeely Memorial Swimming Pool, in 1958, and the foundation contributes to the pool to this day, helping to cover its operating costs so that individuals and families can swim affordably.[9]

Today the McFeely-Rogers Foundation has sixteen million dollars in assets, and those dollars are dedicated almost entirely to the community of Latrobe, supporting recreation, music education, art, historic preservation, and community development efforts. And the foundation's work is still carried out by the McFeely-Rogers extended family. Nancy Rogers was its first president, and Fred was the second. Fred's sister, Laney (whose full name was Nancy Elaine Crozier), also served as president before her death in March of 2019. Jim Okonak, the director, who has been a part of the foundation's work since 1973, is Jim and Nancy's great-nephew, and he hopes his son will take over his work one day.

The offering of self to community was in Fred's very DNA. Caring for the community—for the neighborhood—was what his parents had always done, and it was what Fred would do too. Even as his neighborhood grew—that is, as he moved to Pittsburgh and gained a whole host of television neighbors, first regionally, then nationally—Latrobe remained close to his heart and a focus of his service. Latrobe still claims Fred as its own, perhaps especially because he never stopped claiming Latrobe. Years after his death, his work there—and the work of his parents, who have been gone for decades—continues. The swimming pool and the musical instruments and the art program are as much Fred's legacy as the 895 episodes of *Mister Rogers' Neighborhood*. And the commitment to those neighborhood goods is as deeply a part of who he was as "It's a beautiful day in the neighborhood."

————————————

Fred called Latrobe "the garden spot of the world."[10] I don't know exactly what he meant by that, though it probably had to do with the city's picturesque quality and its lush, hilly surroundings. But the description seems apt in another way as well. Latrobe was a kind of Eden to Fred. It was the place of his own beginning, for one. It also represented an ideal for him, serving as archetypal neighborhood for the man who went on to dream and build and embody a neighborhood so broad as to welcome millions. The long arc of the Christian Scriptures begins in the Garden of Eden and ends with a new heaven and a new earth, the center of which is a city. Fred too left the "garden spot of the world" and, after a few stops along the way, arrived in a city—this one only forty miles from his birthplace—where he began to build his new neighborhood, based in large part on the one that gave him life and breath in the beginning.

Fred was a product of parents whose lives were built around service, and he was a product of a city that valued neighborliness, care for one another, and provision for the downtrodden. It is no wonder that he went out into the world looking for a place to serve, and that the place through which he enacted that service was a neighborhood of his own creation. *Mister Rogers' Neighborhood* took all that was best about Latrobe, Pennsylvania, in the 1920s, '30s, and '40s and built it into a neighborhood for everyone. It's no coincidence that Picture Picture, the friendly, film-showing frame on Mister Rogers's living room wall, so frequently showed films about how things were made. Fred Rogers, son and grandson of industrialists, knew something about the importance of factories, and it was of utmost importance to him that children know that it is *people* who make things. (Even the Neighborhood of Make-Believe had a factory that manufactured rocking chairs and other items.) The entire television neighborhood—full of artists, craftspeople, business owners, and neighborhood helpers—was Fred Rogers's Latrobe, enhanced by his own wide imagination. Latrobe created Fred Rogers; and then Fred Rogers grew up, moved away, and created a kind of Latrobe.

The biblical story of the Garden of Eden is not just a story of beginnings or of an idyll. It is the story of a fall. Present-day Latrobe, though certainly not a fallen ruin, is a city that seems to embody paradox: parking spots are all metered as if in high demand, but the majority of them are empty; streets are one-way, as if to manage great flows of traffic, but those streets are mostly quiet. There are plenty of boarded-up storefronts and spaces for rent, but the city doesn't feel deserted; there are also plenty of businesses that have been holding their own for decades, and others that are new and thriving. Latrobe gives the distinct impression that it had a heyday and that that heyday has passed, but it also has an unmistakable, stubborn, steady hum.

Latrobe is a very American town with a certain kind of American story. It was incorporated in 1854 and grew slowly over its first fifty years. In the first half of the twentieth century, several steel companies emerged, along with a woolen mill, a ceramics company, and a mattress factory. Coal mines, steel mills, and the railroad were major employers in Latrobe, as were the variety of steadily growing downtown businesses and stores.[11] Latrobe was booming, and its population peaked in 1960. But then, as was the case in so many parts of the country, the winds changed. Companies were sold to corporate owners in far-flung cites. Factories closed. Workers lost their jobs, and families moved away. Unemployment numbers climbed. Over decades, businesses shuttered and buildings fell into disrepair. Walmart and Dollar General moved in.

Today's Latrobe is peppered with historical placards and commemorative signs. Some of those signs celebrate Arnold Palmer, the famed and much-beloved golfer who was born in Latrobe. Fred Rogers is everywhere, from the fountain in the park memorializing his father to the sculpture of Fred on the bench looking out over the city. There's even a tiny Trolley on every street sign. "We were pretty proud people here," Jim Okonak said recently. "I used to say, 'Fred Rogers, Arnold Palmer, Rolling Rock beer'—that covers everybody."[12] But, Jim pointed out, Fred died in 2003. Arnold Palmer died in 2016. And Rolling Rock moved to New Jersey in 2006. Latrobe is grieving. It is trying to remember what it once was so that it can figure out what it is.

And maybe this is exactly right. Maybe this is the memory of Eden that leads, eventually, to the city of new creation. Fred's life revealed his hope in this long arc of God's story, as he worked toward new creation on two fronts: investing, practically and emotionally, in the preservation and revitalization of his hometown neighborhood, and all the while making programs for the *Neighborhood* that bore his name.

3

ADOLESCENCE AND ACCEPTANCE

I like you as you are.

Though it can't be said of many people, adolescence was pretty good to Fred Rogers. "Fat Freddy" stretched out—not just physically but also socially. He had always had a rich life at home, playing toy soldiers or puppets or make-believe in the playroom that took up most of the third floor of the Rogers home, learning to play the organ and the piano, listening to radio shows and reading books.[1] But in high school, Fred discovered the power of friendship to affirm, and the power of affirmation to encourage and connect.

When Fred was a freshman in high school, he learned that a classmate named Jim Stumbaugh had been hospitalized following an injury. Jim was a football and basketball player, popular and attractive, a big man on campus, especially compared to the slightly odd, extremely shy, somewhat bullied kid who was terrified to go to school every day for fear of failure. Fred told the story different ways in different contexts: at times, he said that someone asked him to take Jim his schoolwork; in other moments, he confessed, "I don't know why, but something prompted me to take his homework to him in the hospital."[2] (Fred had grown up watching his mother log volunteer hours and his father quietly care for struggling families, so this impulse would have come naturally.) Though Jim later recalled that he "couldn't imagine why Fred Rogers was bringing [him his] homework," he received Fred graciously every day.[3] And the boys began talking.

Over the time Jim was recuperating, he and Fred built a real friendship. "I learned to trust him and told him some of my deepest feelings," Fred recounted at the 1996 Latrobe High School baccalaureate service, "and he told me about his dad's dying two years before and what that was like for him and his mom."[4]

Jim returned to school and told their classmates, "That Rogers kid is OK." And he began to invite Fred along when he and his friends made plans. Fred grew in friendship—and in confidence. In his last two years of high school, thanks to Jim Stumbaugh's acceptance, Fred cultivated an active social life, even hosting parties at his family's country home on the outskirts of town, where they had Latrobe's first in-ground swimming pool.[5] By the time he was a senior in high school, he was editor of the class yearbook, president of the student council, and was voted by his class "Most Likely to Succeed." He graduated salutatorian of his class, and the valedictorian, a young woman named Doris Stewart, was his girlfriend.[6] (Doris lived a few blocks down Weldon Street from the Rogers family with her mother, Marguerite Stewart, who had welcomed the flustered Freddy into her home on that terrifying day almost ten years before.)

Fred and Jim were lifelong friends. Fred was the best man at Jim's wedding, and, though they lived in different parts of the country, they wrote letters and visited when they could.[7]

When Jim was dying of cancer in 1995, Fred traveled out of state with a broken ankle to see him.[8]

"What a difference one person can make in the life of another," Fred said, remembering Jim's willingness to see and embrace who Fred was at his core. With a slight smile, he added, "It's almost as if he said, 'I like you just the way you are.'"[9]

"I like you just the way you are" is a core affirmation of *Mister Rogers' Neighborhood*, where it is spoken (or sung) in hundreds of episodes, including the very first one.

> I like you as you are
> Exactly and precisely
> I think you turned out nicely
> And I like you as you are
>
> I like you as you are
> Without a doubt or question
> Or even a suggestion
> 'Cause I like you as you are
>
> I like your disposition
> Your facial composition
> And with your kind permission
> I'll shout it to a star
>
> I like you as you are
> I wouldn't want to change you
> Or even rearrange you
> Not by far

I like you
I L-I-K-E Y-O-U
I like you, yes I do
I like you, Y-O-U
I like you, like you as you are[10]

Fred's message of unconditional acceptance stemmed not only from the transformative friendship he shared with Jim Stumbaugh but also from his Christian faith, which he discussed in a 1976 radio broadcast he produced for *The Protestant Hour*:

Christianity to me is a matter of being accepted as we are. Jesus certainly wasn't concerned about people's stations in life or what they looked like or whether they were perfect in behavior or feeling. How often in the New Testament we read of Jesus's empathy for those people who felt their own lives to be imperfect, and the marvelous surprise and joy when they sensed his great acceptance.[11]

Indeed, the Judeo-Christian story begins with acceptance and affirmation. In the very first chapter of the Hebrew Bible, God creates the heavens and the earth. Throughout the creation story, the writer notes the goodness of the light, the land and water, the plants, the sun, moon, and stars, and the animals: "God saw how good it was" (Gen. 1:25, CEB). Then, on the sixth day of creation, God creates humans, surveys all that God has made, and sees that it is "*supremely* good" (Gen. 1:31, CEB, emphasis added). Or as Fred sometimes put it, "the bedrock of our being is very good stuff."[12] This foundational belief not only offers divine affirmation but also defends against undue self-doubt. "When we hear the word that we are not lovable," Fred wrote in 1979, "we are *not* hearing the word of

God. No matter how unlovely, how impure or weak or false we may feel ourselves to be, all through the ages God has still called us lovable."[13]

––––––––––––––

Fred seems to have craved affirmation—both human and divine—throughout his life. Writer Tom Junod once followed Fred and the *Neighborhood* crew through New York City and Penn Station, where they were filming a segment for the program. As usual, people approached Fred in droves, and at first, the producer tried to keep them away from him,

> but every time she turned around, there was Mister Rogers putting his arms around someone, or wiping the tears off someone's cheek, or passing around the picture of someone's child, or getting on his knees to talk to a child. . . . After a while, Margy just rolled her eyes and gave up, because it's always like this with Mister Rogers, because the thing that people don't understand about him is that he's *greedy* for this—greedy for the grace that people offer him.[14]

Even after cultivating lifelong friends like Jim Stumbaugh, even after becoming one of the most recognizable, beloved figures of his time, "the need was always there," Joanne said of Fred, "for being loved, for being capable of being loved."[15] Fred knew that he was not the only one who carried this kind of hunger, and so he made it the guiding principle and central message of his program: you are loved, you are loved, you are loved—and you are capable of loving.

The *Neighborhood* received thousands of letters, many of them expressing gratitude for his care. One child's letter to Mister Rogers began "I love your show very much, and I also love you. You are very cute." Then, tellingly, she wrote, "You are my greatest fan."[16]

A twenty-year-old college student wrote Mister Rogers to say that she had recently arrived home for the summer only to find herself

> on the verge of collapse due to exams, play rehears-als, hay fever, a cold and general exhaustion. Con-sequently, for the last three days, the extent of my travels have been from my bed to the livingroom couch. When I couldn't lose myself in unconscious-ness, or amuse myself any other way, I resorted to the television. . . . Your show happened to be on at the time. I just had to write and tell you that Mis-ter Rogers' Neighborhood is really a most delightful experience! When I'm sick I become such a finicky, cranky, temperamental 2 yr. old; and when the atten-tion I demand isn't showered all over me, I get mad and depressed. But to have you come on and be really glad to see *me* . . . you made my day![17]

Fred also frequently received letters from parents, espe-cially mothers, who were grateful for his care not only for their children but also for *them*. In 1973, a woman named Anna wrote to say what his program had meant to her. "I feel like a schoolgirl writing her first love letter," she began. "I know I'm going to mess it all up, say it wrong, forget half of what I had planned—you name it, if it's rotten, I'll do it. But here you are anyway."

She went on to say that she had been watching the *Neigh-borhood* with her children for four years and so appreciated the conversations it allowed her to have with them. Three paragraphs in, she shared more about herself.

I am 30, blind, not much of a housekeeper . . . my children play in the diningroom near me, instead of upstairs 'out of the way.' . . .

I am really enjoying educational TV—"Sesame Street" is busy and boisterous and sometimes angry, but fun. But it is the gentler "Neighborhood" which sustains me . . . because it is my gentler side which weakens first.[18]

In other words, Fred's care worked. To the best of his ability, Fred offered the kind of affirmation he believed God gives to all of us, the kind that Jim Stumbaugh had given to him. He struggled, sometimes, to know it was true for himself, but still he offered it, in faith, to any adoring child or worn-out college student or self-critical parent who might tune in. "I like you just the way you are," he said. ("You are supremely good," he might've added.) And they heard him.

4

COLLEGE YEARS, LONELINESS,
AND MUSICAL EXPRESSION

I'm learning to sing a sad song when I'm sad.

During his senior year of high school, Fred took flying lessons at the Latrobe Airport (now Arnold Palmer Regional Airport) from a young man named George Allen (more on George in chapter 13). Fred enjoyed flying so much that he considered becoming an airline pilot. But he also loved languages, particularly French, and his widening view on the world led him to consider work in the diplomatic corps. In the fall of 1946, he headed off to Dartmouth to pursue this path, majoring in romance languages.

But according to Maxwell King's biography of Fred, he was miserable at Dartmouth.[1] He had left Latrobe, where he was finally flourishing, only to land in a place that he later remembered as being "very cold."[2] King suggests that Fred was uncomfortable in the school's party culture: for all his social successes in high school, Fred was still conservative and shy.

In emotional turmoil, lonely and wrong-footed, Fred did exactly what he did when he was eight: he turned to music to express what he felt. He still loved learning and speaking French (he had discovered in high school that languages offered outlets for emotion too; "I used to be able to say things in French that I could never say in English!"[3]), but he longed for music. In his second year at Dartmouth he approached Arnold Kvam, who had been recently hired to develop a music major at the college, and he received some surprising advice. "Fred, we won't have this department ready for you in the four years that you'll be here," Fred recalled him saying. "Why don't you take a look at the place that I just came from, which is Rollins College."[4]

Easter vacation was coming, so Fred planned a visit to Rollins. It would prove to be the first of two deeply significant Easter vacations in his life, each of which was something of a resurrection for Fred (the second would come three years later; see chapter 5). When he landed in Florida, a group of Rollins students, including Joanne Byrd, the eventual Mrs. Rogers, met him at the airport. They were in a "wonderful old car," Joanne remembers. "And we were hanging out the window when he came out—and [we] grabbed him, and just took him right with us and made him one of us. And he just blended in so well."[5]

The students showed Fred the campus, including the music conservatory, where, Joanne recalls, Fred "sat right down and started playing some pop stuff. And we were so impressed, because none of us could do that. We couldn't just sit down and play jazz. And he could. He could do it all."[6]

"Rollins was very warm," Fred remembered, recalling his visit, "and I just felt so much at home there. And so, the next year, I went to Rollins."[7]

Fred majored in music composition and minored in French, and he made a number of lifelong friends: Joanne Byrd (Rogers), of course, and her piano-performance partner Jeannine Morrison, as well as John Reardon, a baritone who would go on to sing with the Metropolitan Opera in New York City and appear in over fifty *Neighborhood* episodes, especially during opera weeks. A recent write-up from Rollins recalls that Fred "was active at the College, serving on the chapel staff and as a member of the Community Service Club, the Student Music Guild, the French Club, the Welcoming Committee, the After Chapel Club, and the Alpha Phi Lambda fraternity. He also sang in the chapel and Bach choirs."[8] Fred competed in intramural swimming at Rollins too,[9] and he chaired the Interfaith and Race Relations Committee, a group that provided funds and services for nearby African American communities.[10]

"Life is for service," read a marble engraving near one of the halls on campus. Fred, known among his friends as something of a jokester, often covered part of the sign so it read, "Life is for vice."[11] Still, this straightforward message impressed Fred enough that he wrote it on a slip of paper and carried it in his wallet for many years. Later, a Rollins professor framed a photograph of the engraving and gifted it to Fred, and he kept it in his office at WQED, the Pittsburgh television station where he spent most of his career.[12]

———————————

The 2018 documentary *Won't You Be My Neighbor?* includes an archival clip in which Fred calls music "my first language." When five-year-old Freddy asked for a pump organ that cost twenty-five dollars,[13] his grandfather McFeely agreed to match whatever money Freddy earned toward that goal. Some sources say that the affectionate Ding Dong gave in and bought the organ after Fred had earned his first dollar.[14] Others suggest that Fred's McFeely grandparents bought him the organ as a reward for making it through that summer of air-conditioned confinement when he was five.[15] Fred's grandmother McFeely, whom he called Nana, bought him his own piano when he was almost ten.[16] Eventually, she also bought him a Hammond organ, and he began learning to play with feet as well as hands.[17] At Christmastime Fred's father would put the organ's speaker cabinet on the front steps of their house while Fred played carols for the neighborhood.[18]

Fred was clearly gifted in music from a young age—he could play well by ear, and he was a quick study. Very early on, music began to carry a meaning in his life that his other important hobbies—his puppet play and photography, hosting friends and helping in the community—could not touch. When he was bullied at age eight, he explored his grief at the piano. When he felt angry at having to suddenly share his parents' affections with a sibling at age eleven, he pounded the keys. Joanne has noted that both she and Fred grew up in emotionally reticent families,[19] and on his program, Mister Rogers once shared with his television neighbors that his parents didn't like for him to act out when he was mad—to stomp or hit things. "But I found that if I played the piano when I was angry, they didn't mind that, so that's what I did."[20] Fred was a person of deep and intricate feeling, and music was his first and best way to express whatever he felt; he "laughed and cried through his fingers," as he put it.[21] "There's something very mystical and wonderful about how music can touch us," he once said.[22]

At Dartmouth, perhaps Fred found himself wandering, again and again, to pianos, where he could work through his feelings of inner conflict and homesickness. It's easy to imagine such a practice, in a lonely time, leading him toward the deeper study of music that he would find at Rollins.

Turning to music in times of intense feeling was deep in Fred's religious DNA. The book of Psalms in the Hebrew Bible was used in worship as early as five hundred years before the time of Jesus, and Jesus himself quotes from several psalms in the Gospels, including his cry of dereliction on the cross—"My God, my God, why have you forsaken me?" (Matt. 27:46, NRSV)—which references Psalm 22. It's clear that the psalms involved music: many include instructions for musicians or musical leaders (see, for example, Psalm 4, which says, "For the music leader: With stringed instruments," or Psalm 5, "For the music leader: For the flutes"). Many congregations still sing psalms in worship, including Latrobe Presbyterian Church, which Fred attended throughout his childhood.

The psalms are a rich read for all sorts of reasons. They're beautiful, sophisticated poetry, for one. They also have catechetical purposes, teaching the stories *of* God's people *to* God's people, in ways they can recall together again and again. The psalms craft powerful, creative metaphors, like God as a sheltering bird under whose wings one can find refuge (Psalm 91). But one of the psalms' greatest gifts—one certainly not lost on Fred—is the vast range of human emotion and experience they represent. While there are psalms of pure praise, brimming with joy and worship of God (for example, Psalm 150), many more psalms give voice to feelings of loneliness (Psalm 88), fear (Psalm 22), grief (Psalm 6), and anger (Psalm 137)—right alongside their verses of praise.

Hebrew Scripture makes room for every kind of feeling, and it sets these feelings to music. When Freddy the bullied, chased child took refuge at the piano, and likewise Fred the homesick collegiate, he was participating in an ancient tradition of expressing raw emotion through music. The content of the psalms indicates that God and God's people have blessed emotional expression for thousands of years. Fred heard the cue and joined the song.

———————

Throughout his life, Fred used music to express how he felt, and in his years on the *Neighborhood*, he invited his television neighbors into that practice (see chapter 16). Having found his way into self-expression at the piano, Fred wanted to share ways of expressing feeling—musical and otherwise. This became a key part of his ministry with children and families as he urged them to offer their full, honest selves to the world.

5

FORMATION IN NEW YORK CITY

You're growing.

In the spring of 1951, Fred was wrapping up his final semester at Rollins College and planning to start seminary in the fall. But when he went home for Easter break, he encountered a recent family purchase that would change his postcollege trajectory: a television set, one of the first in town. As he and his family flipped through the channels, they came across a children's program.

Throughout his life, Fred often told the story of what happened next. "I saw people throwing pies at each other's faces, and that to me was such demeaning behavior. And if there's anything that bothers me, it's one person demeaning another."[1] Somehow, right away, Fred knew two things. First, he knew he found this kind of children's programming not just distasteful but destructive; it failed to take children seriously, and, even worse, it insulted them. Second, he knew this failing wasn't inherent to television as a medium; he intuited television's capacity for extraordinary good. "I thought, this could be a wonderful tool for education. Why is it being used this way? And so I said to my parents, 'You know, I don't think I'll go to seminary right away. I think maybe I'll go into television. And they said, 'Why, you've never even seen it!' And I said, 'Well, I've seen enough of it here.'"[2]

Despite their initial surprise at his pronouncement, Fred's parents came around to supporting their son. Fred's father used his connections to help him land a job at NBC in New York. Fred started work on October 1, 1951, and stayed with NBC for the next two years. Fred's transition into television work and into his New York years thus began with a significant "yes" and a significant "no": yes to television and no to seminary—at least for now. Indeed, the two years Fred Rogers spent in New York, the first two years of his television career, were full of significant choices—yeses and noes that would shape Fred's entire life and continue to form him into the person we would later know as Mister Rogers.

———————

People who study theology or liturgy or religious education like to use the word *formation* to talk about how the things we do again and again—kneel, sing, pray, receive the bread and wine—actually shape us into who we are. We are molded by our actions and our rituals, religious and quotidian alike; the shape we take in each moment has everything to do with what we have spent all our previous moments doing.

Fred Rogers's choices in New York seem to have been particularly formative for him. It's hard to say whether he had an inherent knowledge of how those choices would matter later—which would be rare for a twenty-something recent graduate—or if his early decisions just happened to set him on an extraordinary path. Either way, those early days—those early choices—mattered deeply for Fred and for the millions of people who would come to make up his audience.

Even before Fred's "yes" to television transplanted him to New York, he said another quiet, formative "no" in response to pies in faces: "no" to whatever was the reigning television gimmick of the day. Throughout his almost fifty years in television, Fred said no to every voice (perhaps even some internal ones) that told him that to do such and such would generate better ratings or bigger profits: "no" to picking up the pace; "no" to animation; "no" to licensing of merchandise; "no" to moving *Mister Rogers' Neighborhood* to network television, or even to a bigger city like New York or Los Angeles. And as he said no to greater speed, more money, and higher ratings, he said yes to quieter goods: thoughtfulness, intentionality, and his own intuition and imagination for the work, those very same values that pointed him, that second life-changing Easter, toward television as a force for greater good—and, yes, toward New York.

When Fred moved to New York City, Joanne Byrd was at Florida State University in Tallahassee working on her master's degree in piano performance.[3] She and Fred had been close friends all through college and attended some dances together. "I suppose our friends probably thought of us as 'a couple,'" she recalled.[4] But when Joanne graduated a year before Fred (their ages differ by only a few days, but Fred was a year behind Joanne in school due to his transfer from Dartmouth), their relationship remained undefined. They kept in touch, particularly through letters, while also moving forward with their separate lives. But then one day Joanne received a letter from Fred proposing marriage. She considered briefly, then ran to the nearest phone booth to call and accept his proposal.[5]

Fred called Joanne "such a joyful person," full of laughter, and Nicholas Ma, producer of *Won't You Be My Neighbor?*, shared in a recent interview that Joanne, now in her nineties, is an avid texter. "Not only does she text, but she loves emojis. . . . Anytime there's good news about the film, she sends a heart emoji with an exclamation point. That's kind of a great way to describe Joanne as a person: a heart with an exclamation point."[6] Joanne's gregarious humor and easy warmth were a welcome gift to introspective, serious Fred.

Joanne brings a nurturing quality to her relationships— even, at times, with near strangers. In the early months of their marriage, while Fred was working on a Leonard Bernstein opera called *Trouble in Tahiti* at NBC, the lead became upset and announced that she would no longer play the part. The crew was stunned: "It was scheduled to be broadcast that night . . . and everything was live then." So Joanne took the lead back to their apartment, made tea for her, and listened to her complaints. By showtime, the star was "somehow, magically" costumed, made up, and ready for action. Telling this story in a 2000 interview, Fred said, by way of explanation, "Joanne is a *wonderful* person."[7]

Fred and Joanne had music in common from the very beginning. Joanne was a touring concert pianist for many years, most often playing in a two-piano act with Jeannine Morrison. In letters and emails to friends, Fred regularly shared where and what Joanne was playing next: "Joanne flies into Atlanta around noon today."[8] "Joanne just called from Athens, Ohio, where she and Jeannine will give a master class tomorrow."[9] "Joanne and Jeannine played in Palm Beach late yesterday afternoon. Evidently the pianos were not the best (to say the least). . . . At any rate I'm sure that J&J did their best with what was given to them. Their personalities let them rise above poor instruments."[10]

Later in life, Fred and Joanne downsized to a modest apartment, but they always had two grand pianos in their living room.[11]

Joanne's joy, her nurturing presence, her music: when he penned his proposal letter, Fred said yes to all of it—a yes that he would keep saying throughout their fifty years of marriage, each time becoming more deeply formed by it. Happily, Sara Joanne Byrd said yes right back to him.

When Fred began working in New York at age twenty-three, he was an assistant to the producer of the *NBC Television Opera Theatre*, and this often meant he was given small errands to run, including fetching refreshments for the talent and for others higher up the ladder than he. One day, he brought coffee to someone (he declined to reveal the person's name in the interview) who took one sip and said curtly, "I wanted milk and not sugar."

"I just felt crestfallen," Fred said, his dismay evident. "When you serve people—Cokes and coffees and whatever they might want—you see what people are like."[12]

As Fred's public persona evolved over the years following his gopher days at NBC—"I mean, who would've ever thought that somebody would want my autograph or want to take my picture?"[13]—he always remembered how it felt to be treated with disdain by someone with power. And those who spent time with him in public testify that he always stopped to share a kind word with people who sought his attention or offered him care—sometimes to the point of annoyance. Fred's friend and pastor John McCall remembered that people would constantly stop Fred on the street or approach him in public places, so much so that McCall sometimes dreaded this aspect of going out with Fred. "It was irritating to me after a while because I found it intrusive," he said, "but Fred did not get impatient."[14]

Fred felt great ambivalence about fame. He once said that the most difficult thing he ever did was walk across the *Neighborhood* set that first time and sing, "It's a beautiful day in the neighborhood."[15] His good friend Christopher de Vinck recalled that Fred would share his high-profile appearances and greatest honors only obliquely. "I'm going to go to California to do a little TV work," he might say when he was going to appear on *The Tonight Show*, or "Joanne and I are going to spend a few days in Washington, DC," when he was going to receive the Presidential Medal of Freedom.[16] From the very beginning, since working for the stars on the NBC sets in New York, Fred Rogers said no to the entitlements of fame.

———————

Fred may have said no to seminary, for a time, when he decided to move to New York, but he continued to say yes to God with as much dedication as ever. He began stopping by St. Patrick's Cathedral to pray in the mornings on his way to NBC.[17]

Meanwhile, when he had time off, he would spend it in daycare centers, orphanages, and hospitals, visiting with children.[18] "And I cannot tell you why," he told Terry Gross in a 1985 interview, reflecting back. "I'm sure it had very deep roots."[19] He was beginning to sense a direction for his life, and he was saying yes to it in the ways he knew how, but the contours of his future vocation were still a mystery to him.

Because of his music degree, Fred was assigned to work mostly on music and variety shows at NBC: *The Kate Smith Hour*, *NBC Television Opera Theatre*, *Your Hit Parade*, and *The Voice of Firestone*. He also worked, for a time, as floor manager of *The Gabby Hayes Show*. Gabby Hayes was an actor who played comic sidekicks in nearly two hundred western films in the 1930s and '40s. His 1969 *New York Times* obituary remembered him like this: "With his rum-sodden, cantankerous disposition, his Buffalo Bill coiffure, his whiskers and his rags, Gabby Hayes personified the movies' notion of the Old Man of the Wild West. . . . When he appeared on screen, his fans knew they were in the land of identifiable good guys and bad guys."[20]

The Gabby Hayes Show, which Fred Rogers floor-managed in the early 1950s, was a familiar format for the time: Hayes would enter in costume and introduce a western film, which would then play. Hayes might return in the middle of the show to address the audience again, and then, following the film, Hayes would return and say goodbye. Fred was a good floor manager, engaged and attentive when Hayes was on camera. Fred remembered Hayes saying to him, "Do you realize that you're the only face that I see? . . . It makes such a difference if [the] floor manager seems interested in what you're doing."[21]

Fred *was* interested. He asked Hayes one day, "Mr. Hayes, what do you think of when you look at that camera and know that there are thousands of people watching you?"

And Fred never forgot Hayes's reply: "Freddy, I think of one little buckaroo."

Though Fred always insisted that being on camera himself hadn't yet crossed his mind during those New York years, Hayes's words formed him deeply enough to remain with him all his life. "You know, that must've gone straight to my heart," he reflected, "because when I look at the camera, I think of one person. Not any specific person, but one person." Fred was already saying yes to intimate connection through television. "It's very, very personal, this medium."[22]

In 1953, Fred heard from his father that plans were in the works in Pittsburgh, only forty miles from Latrobe, to start the first community-based public television station in the United States.[23] He was eager to learn more. "I told some of my friends at NBC that I thought I'd put my name in and apply for the station."

But his New York friends were appalled. "They said, 'You are nuts! That place isn't even on the air yet, and you're in line to be a producer or a director or anything you want to be here.' And I said, 'No, I have the feeling that educational television might be, at least for me, the way of the future.'"[24]

So Fred applied and was accepted, making him one of the first six people to be hired at WQED. He and Joanne moved to Pittsburgh in November 1953, and WQED went on the air in April of the following year. And so Fred said yes to educational television while at the same time saying no to upward mobility. As a result, he had the chance to be on the ground floor of a new venture, one where he hoped he could use even more of his gifts in the service of education through this medium whose power, now, he had seen firsthand and whose intricacies, now, he had learned from the other side of the camera.

The personal and professional formation Fred underwent, especially in his first few years out of college, contributed to his depth, steadiness, and self-assurance. Those qualities were part of what gave him an unusual magnetism, one strong enough to convey across the medium of television. What Fred Rogers experienced and chose over time, again and again, formed him into who he was, just as each person's day-to-day experiences and choices create the person who will live—and experience and choose—tomorrow. The man who left New York for Pittsburgh was growing, day by day, into the person millions of Americans would come to know as Mister Rogers.

6

WHIMSY AND SERIOUSNESS
ON *THE CHILDREN'S CORNER*

It's a neighborly day in this beauty wood.

When Karen Herman interviewed Fred Rogers in 1999 for the Archive of American Television, she asked him about his work at WQED, the Pittsburgh educational television station he helped to start in 1953. He began to tell her the story of *The Children's Corner*, a local program that ran from 1954 to 1961. Josie Carey was the host of the show, and Fred's job was to produce it and to play the organ. Soon, almost by accident, he also became the show's puppeteer.

"Daniel Tiger made his appearance the very first day," Fred explained. The program was live, and it was on for a full hour, so Fred and Josie used the puppets to fill the time, especially when their other plans fell through, like when the films broke for the free movies they frequently showed, or when their special guests only filled ten minutes instead of thirty. Daniel was such a hit, Fred recalled, that they began to introduce other puppets.

"I had this king puppet at home," he told Karen in the interview, and as he told her this, Fred found King Friday and placed him on his hand. "His name was King Friday XIII, and he was very sad because he had lost his country." Here, King Friday himself chimed in to tell the story: "I said to the people, would you kindly suggest a name for my new country?" Fred continued, telling Karen that one child wrote in to suggest the name Calendarland. As Fred spoke, King Friday turned to watch and listen to him. Then the king turned back to the camera and continued in his haughty voice, "Yes, so that boy, we called that boy and said, you may come to Calendarland, and I will make you a prince."

As Fred continued sharing his memories of the early days of *The Children's Corner*, he began to reach toward the puppet, to take him off his hand. But he hesitated, and King Friday interrupted to say, "If you'll excuse me, I have an important meeting."

"Yes," Fred replied.

"Yes, excuse me, Karen," King Friday said, bowing toward the interviewer and the camera. Then Fred removed the puppet from his hand, put it away, and turned back to the camera himself. Only then did his face break into a grin. "Here we're back to whimsy," he said. And he opened his mouth wide and laughed.

From the time he was a young child, Fred Rogers was a whimsical soul. During his long days of childhood illness, he would sit in bed and make up stories, his toys climbing the mountains made by his knees under the blankets.[1] But he was also, from the time of his earliest memories, a serious soul, interior and thoughtful, exploring life's deep questions and big feelings with his puppets or at his piano. Both whimsy and seriousness were rooted deep in Fred, and both, for him, were theological, growing out of his belief that all of God's created world—both its whimsy and its seriousness—is good. From 1953 to 1961, Fred worked on *The Children's Corner*, a program characterized by whimsy; meanwhile, behind the scenes, in his own mind and in conversation with Josie Carey, he sometimes found his seriousness in a wrestling match with the whimsy he so loved. The external fruit of these *Corner* years is easy to see: Fred and Josie not only produced a wildly popular show; they also developed many of the skills, songs, and characters that Fred would use on the *Neighborhood*. But the internal work of this time was also crucial, as Fred negotiated, in himself, the relationship between the seriousness and whimsy that were both so integral to his being.

In 1953, when Fred and Joanne Rogers moved to Pittsburgh, Fred was tasked with putting a program schedule together at WQED. A month before the station was to go on the air, Dorothy Daniel, the station's general manager (and Daniel Striped Tiger's namesake), pointed out that there was no children's program in the works. She asked for volunteers, and Fred stepped up, along with Josie Carey, an actress who was working as a secretary at the station. Fred and Josie had one month to develop their program, which became *The Children's Corner.*[2]

The format was straightforward: Josie would greet the viewers and sing a few songs with Fred accompanying on organ. Then she would introduce their film or guest for the day. She would also manage transitions and close the show. Each hour-long show would be live, and shows would run five days a week.

"Well, can you imagine producing an hour a day?" Fred asked, recalling the enormous workload. "Can you imagine the amount of material you'd need for an hour a day? . . . The puppets, I think, saved us."[3]

In time, many of the puppets familiar to viewers of *Mister Rogers' Neighborhood* got their start on *The Children's Corner*: not only Daniel Striped Tiger and King Friday XIII but also Henrietta Pussycat, X the Owl, and Lady Elaine Fairchilde. Josie and Fred developed the puppets' storylines gradually, as they ad-libbed their show, day after day. Daniel, for example, was a tiger who had recently become tame. He became the leader of the Tame Tiger Torganization, which children who watched the program could join, earning stripes for particular accomplishments. When X the Owl flew into town and decided to stay, he didn't have a tree to live in, so the others suggested he find an acorn and plant it. Each day following, the art crew painted a little higher up the set so that the tree seemed to grow, over the course of a week or two, into a full-size oak.[4]

As the stories developed, so did Fred's skills. Josie remembered that he used to gargle water to get Daniel's voice right; it had a slight growl to it at the time, though it (and Daniel himself) seems to have gentled over the years. Fred also developed his skills as a puppeteer. At the beginning, Josie recalled, the puppets could open and close their arms, perhaps nod their heads. But later, their movements became very subtle and expressive. Once, on air, Josie was holding a pumpkin that belonged to X the Owl. She dropped it accidentally and immediately looked at X, "and I swore his eyes filled with tears."[5]

Josie found herself beginning to trust the puppets, especially Daniel. In his 1999 interview, Fred recalled an afternoon when Josie was distraught. Something that had happened earlier in the day was weighing heavily on her, and she said to Daniel, on air, "Daniel, I'm so upset!" Daniel replied, "Well, you just tell me about it."

"And she just bared her soul to him," Fred marveled. "I wonder if she even knew that we were on the air and the camera was on—she probably did. But she trusted Daniel's ears so, and she trusted her audience so, that she could be her whole self."[6]

This kind of intimate conversation between Daniel and Josie became a regular feature of the program. "I would get so engrossed in the conversation," Josie said, "that after it was over, I'd go around the back of the set and tell Fred what Daniel had said to me."[7]

Josie and Fred always had a clever, easy chemistry on air. Josie remembered, "Fred and I just . . . the gears all met. It was wonderful. From the very moment we said hello."[8] They were also a formidable songwriting team—Josie usually wrote the words, and then Fred wrote the music. Josie found Fred's knack for melodies both delightful and infuriating: "He had great taste. . . . He had a wonderful music background, so he wrote these beautiful melodies. I thought I'd died and gone to heaven. . . . I would get so mad though. I would spend hours and hours and hours on a lyric, and I would hand it to Fred. . . . All he had to do was read it through, and he had a melody for it. It was fabulous."[9]

For about a year during the later days of *The Children's Corner*, Fred and Josie would fly to New York on Fridays after doing their fifth Pittsburgh program of the week. They would prep that night, then do an hour-long live show for NBC on Saturday before flying back home to Pittsburgh Saturday night. Often, on the flight from Pittsburgh to New York, Josie and Fred would write a song for the next day's program. Josie also liked the challenge of writing a story or a lyric on the bus or streetcar on the way to work. "We were both very . . . I guess we were creative," she said.[10]

Only one segment of *The Children's Corner* was scripted, and it was called "The Attic" (and recalling it made the seventy-one-year-old Fred Rogers cackle).[11] This attic was filled with items that would come to life and speak to Josie or to each other: Phil O. Dendron (voiced by Fred) and Rhoda Dendron (voiced by Fred's wife, Joanne); Lydia Lamp and Lawrence Light (who eventually got married—a rarely-seen-on-camera Fred Rogers officiating); Foo-Foo Fish (a rubber fish voiced by Josie), and Gramma Phone. A mouse named Teop (*poet* spelled backward) lived in the attic and spoke in rhyme. Characters like Bill Bookworm, Effie the Fire Engine, and Ino A. Horse also made appearances. Several of the characters formed the Attic Cultural Movement Society, a group that listened to opera together and fought one another for the place by the window. Though the segment was scripted, full of puns and whimsy and recurring jokes, it was still performed live, and Fred and Josie and the others relied on high school–age volunteers to make the items move at the right time. Gramma Phone's cabinets would open and close when she spoke, Lydia's lampshade would wiggle, and Lawrence's light would go on and off.[12]

———————

The Children's Corner went on the air the very first day of regular programming on WQED: April 5, 1954.[13] After that first episode, they received sixty-eight pieces of mail from enthusiastic viewers. Three and a half months later, on July 12, they received further affirmation of the program's popularity when they decided to host a birthday party for Daniel Striped Tiger. They announced the party on the air and invited any children who had earned four stripes in the Tame Tiger Torganization to come and celebrate with Daniel during the show on his birthday. They prepared cake, ice cream, and punch for a few dozen children, but when they looked out the window an hour before showtime, they saw a line of children and parents stretching all the way around the block. There were so many children that they filled not only the studio but also the gallery (a glassed-in balcony overhead for viewing whatever was happening in the studio) and the yard outside. Staff members quickly cut each piece of cake into four, split each serving of ice cream into four, and asked kids to choose only one thing—cake, ice cream, or punch. And then the program began.

To earn the fourth stripe in the Tame Tiger Torganization, children were supposed to have learned the club song, "Je suis un tigre apprivoisé," which translates, "I am a tame tiger." The moment came during Daniel's birthday show for all the kids—who supposedly came to the party because they had earned their fourth stripe—to sing the song. Josie assumed they'd fumble their way through and that many of the kids had come without really knowing it—"it's a difficult song!" But Fred played the song's by-then-familiar intro on the organ, and the children began to sing:

> Je suis un tigre apprivoisé.
> Vous êtes un tigre. Vous me plaisez.
> Hamburger pour moi. Hamburger pour vous.
> Hamburger pour tout le monde.
> Soyez un tigre apprivoisé![14]

"They sang as one voice," Josie recalled. "I still get goose-bumps. It was probably the most exciting moment in my career. I really want to tear up even now, thinking of how those children responded."[15]

Fred and Josie had quite a few good years working together, but the schedule was grueling. Fred decided to enter seminary after all, and he began taking courses on his lunch hour. (His slow pace meant that it took him eight years to earn his divinity degree.[16]) He loved his coursework, but when he wrote to his friend Fred Rainsberry in 1960, he was grateful to be approaching Christmas break: "I'm in the middle of term papers and preparation for examinations this and next month, but Seminary gives us a month between semesters . . . ! It'll be nice to live only one life for a while. At the moment I feel that I'd rather have the vacation from the daily program. . . . It's all I can do to think up a new 'Corner' five times a week."[17]

Fred and Josie also began to discover that they had different priorities for children's television. Josie loved to be an entertainer, relishing the camera and the children's laughter. But while he clearly shared Josie's whimsical sense of humor, Fred worried increasingly about the subtler messages children were receiving. He became uncomfortable any time the humor approached slapstick or hinted at anything demeaning, particularly if it treated children's feelings with less than utmost care. He would bring these concerns to Josie following the broadcasts.[18]

Josie remembered an argument over whether to use the word *would*, *could*, or *should* in some particular circumstance. It wasn't really a fight, she clarified. "You'd never fight with Fred. He says, 'Oh no,' and that's the end of that." But "we must've had a twenty-minute discussion over which one was the proper word to use." Their arguments became frequent enough that Fred's mother knew about them, and she found she could tell when they'd been arguing before the program because they would be excessively sweet and kind to each other on the air.[19]

No story shows Fred and Josie's differences as clearly as the story of the monkey finger puppet. Josie starred in multiple other shows during (and after) the run of *The Children's*

Corner. While she was working on a show at KDKA, a commercial Pittsburgh station, a storyline evolved in which a monkey puppet lost his baby, which was a little monkey finger puppet. On the fly—this show, too, was ad-libbed—the puppeteer said that the baby monkey was in the glove compartment of a car, headed to Cleveland. Kids responded well to the storyline; not only did they find it funny, but kids from Cleveland started sending things to the studio with notes asking, "Is this your baby?" Josie found the whole thing very entertaining, and when she went to WQED one afternoon for *The Children's Corner*, she told Fred about it.

"Oh! He was appalled," Josie remembered. She recalled him saying, "Do you realize that is one of the worst things you can tell a child? Why, a child is so afraid of being left or lost! And it's such an enclosed place, the glove compartment, the child is going to feel that he's going to be put into a situation where he's in a small place and he's lost his parents." By this time, Fred was taking courses in child development in cooperation with his seminary courses, and they were affecting the way he viewed childhood and children.

"Hey!" Josie replied. "It's a joke; it's a silly program! The kids know it's silly!"

But Fred's mind would not be changed. "He thought it was just horrible."[20]

Fred himself did not tell this story—or any others like it—when Karen Herman asked him about the ending of *The Children's Corner*. He didn't mention conflict at all. In his telling, Josie was busy with other shows, and he was headed to Canada. His friend Fred Rainsberry had invited him to develop a children's show for the Canadian Broadcasting Corporation, and he was eager for the opportunity. In a 1961 letter to Rainsberry, as these new opportunities were beginning to come into focus, Fred's enthusiasm and relief were palpable:

You'll never know what your telephone call did for
my spirits the other night! It had been a long day of
plannings and doings and I had come home to wonder
if man wasn't really meant to just sit by his own fire
and develop a craft which could be easily carried out
at home. Whittling was very tempting at the moment.
(But I don't know the first thing about whittling.) At any
rate it was starting out to be a reflective evening and
I just couldn't seem to find too much positive reflec-
tion beyond our front door—and THEN YOU CALLED. It
doesn't happen very often, and "chills down the spine"
is a very non-technical word for it; but, as you listed all
of the possible things we might be able to do together,
I got that feeling. I guess it all comes from knowing
that someone you like is thinking about you.[21]

Fred Rogers was a man of whimsy. He loved to create with
it, and he loved to talk about it. Many of his most fertile
creative partnerships were built on a shared love of whimsy.
But for Fred, whimsy was always in conversation with seriousness. During the years he and Josie created *The Children's
Corner*, Fred was figuring out the nature of that conversation:
When should whimsy discard seriousness, and when should
seriousness override whimsy? What does one have to do
with the other? Are they opposite ends of a spectrum? Do
they exist in tension with each other, or can they live side
by side?

Clearly, in Fred's mind, seriousness must sometimes
temper whimsy, as when he felt so passionately that the
lost baby monkey was a worrisome storyline for children.
But whimsy and seriousness, for Fred, were never opposites.
Being serious about children and their emotional needs

never meant he couldn't build a Neighborhood of Make-Believe with a museum-go-round at its center. And being serious about television and its best uses never meant he couldn't write a character who could wish a rainbow into existence or flip the Eiffel Tower upside down with the use of a magical boomerang. For Fred, whimsy and seriousness coexisted.

Perhaps the best way to clarify the relationship between these two values is to say this: Fred Rogers was serious about whimsy. And what's more, he was theological about it. In a class paper he wrote during seminary titled "The Minister and the Young Child," he closed by quoting an essay by Francis Thompson, an English poet, ascetic, and mystic.

> Know you what it is to be a child? It is to be something very different from the man of today. It is to have a spirit yet streaming from the world of baptism; it is to believe in love, to believe in loveliness, to believe in belief; it is to be so little that the elves can reach to whisper in your ear; it is to turn pumpkins into coaches, and mice into horses, lowness into loftiness, and nothing into everything, for each child has its fairy godmother in its own soul; it is to live in a nutshell and to count yourself a king of infinite space; it is
>
> > To see a world in a grain of sand
> > And a heaven in a wild flower,
> > Hold infinity in the palm of your hand
> > And eternity in an hour.[22]

In this excerpt, Thompson links baptism to whimsy. Baptism, a rite that marks a child's belonging to God, is somehow connected not just to "loveliness" and "belief" but also to elves, pumpkins, and fairy godmothers. Belonging to God means baptism into the whimsical world that God has created, both the natural one and the one in our own imaginations—the one in our own neighborhoods of make-believe. And the second is no less God's than the first.

Fred Rogers saw God everywhere—and perhaps this is what made him serious and whimsical in equal measure. He saw God in the open and vulnerable hearts and minds of the children watching his programs, and so he worried about choosing just the right words and storylines to honor the time they and their families had entrusted to him. But he also saw God in children's unencumbered play—the knees making mountains under sheets, the wild imaginings of puppets and playthings. All of it was sacred.

———————————

Fred sent an email to a friend, journalist Tom Junod, on Easter Sunday in 1999. He told Tom that he had celebrated Easter with his grandsons the previous day. They had a conversation, probably initiated by Fred, about the meaning of Easter. Fred—"Babba" to the boys—talked about Jesus's death and resurrection, "and how that means that God loves us."

> "I know something else about Jesus," little Douglas (six years old) piped up.
> "And what is that?" asked his Babba (me).
> "Jesus told the Easter Bunny to bring presents to everybody."
> Well, I could hardly keep a straight face; but I had to since little Douglas told it [with] such seriousness . . . and who knows Jesus might have really done that.[23]

In this exchange, Fred not only takes his grandson's feelings seriously, as we might expect. He takes the whimsy seriously. And because he does, his theological conversation with his grandsons is infused with lightness and joy. Indeed, the whole neighborhood of Fred's life was infused with these qualities—which, he believed, reflect the generous delight of God.

7

GRADUATE STUDIES AND LIFE-TRANSFORMING TEACHERS

Did you know when you marvel, you're learning?

By the time *The Children's Corner* ceased production in 1961, the Tame Tiger Torganization had 150,000 members.[1] During the program's seven-year run, Josie and Fred had written dozens of songs, invented and developed countless characters and storylines, and recorded two albums. By all measures, it had been a great success. During these same years, Fred was in seminary, working slowly toward his divinity degree, and he also began graduate studies in child development. Through his studies he met some of the teachers—and learned from them some of the lessons—that would shape the rest of his life and work.

Fred enrolled at Western Theological Seminary after he'd been working at WQED for about a year. (Western Theological Seminary is now Pittsburgh Theological Seminary after merging with Pittsburgh-Xenia Theological Seminary in 1959.) He knew he could manage only one course at a time, so he asked the admissions staff which class he should take first. "They didn't even hesitate. 'Oh, Bill Orr's systematic theology,' they said unanimously."[2] Fred signed up.

He discovered quickly that Dr. Orr was a vibrant character. "Talk about absentminded," Fred recalled in a 1999 interview. "He'd come into the room—he was a smoker—and he would flick his ash in the wastebasket, and one time it caught fire, and he was lecturing, and he just took his foot," and here Fred himself stomped his foot on the floor, off to the side, "and put the fire out. He didn't skip one syllable; he just kept on talking. Fabulous, fabulous man."[3] But as always, Fred was a close watcher of people, and he began to notice that there was more to this professor than his quirkiness. At his center was a deep well of faith and compassion.

> Oh, we learned about epistemology and Christology and eschatology and sanctification and justification and existentialism, but most of all we witnessed the unfolding of the life of one of God's saints. Dr. Orr would be quick to remind me that we're all saints, we believers; nevertheless, when you see someone go out to lunch on a winter's day and come back without his overcoat because he had given it to a person who was cold, you have a growing understanding of "living theologically." When we asked Dr. Orr about the coat, he said, "Oh, I have one other at home," and that was all he said about it.[4]

Fred was captivated. He took every class he could with Dr. Orr, including postgraduate continuing education courses. He also maintained a friendship with him and his wife, Mildred, visiting them regularly for the rest of their lives. Fred and other students often said that Dr. Orr "loved [them] right through seminary."[5] At Orr's funeral, Fred thanked God for Bill's "love of learning, his generosity with his time, his seemingly uncanny understanding of what others happened to need at any given moment, his great ability to make a foreign language come alive in ways that his students could understand not only in their minds but in their lives, his love of beauty of things seen and unseen, heard and unheard, his patience, and his faith."[6] (The description sounds not a little like Fred Rogers himself.)

For Fred, Bill Orr's theology built on the love of his grandfather—"Freddy, you've made this day a special day for me"—and the affirmation of his high school friend Jim Stumbaugh—"I like you just the way you are." Though Orr "didn't talk about evil very much," when he did, he spoke not of demons or Satan but of "the accuser" and of the way evil operates on the self. "Evil will do anything to make you feel as bad as you possibly can about yourself," Fred recalled Orr teaching, "because if you feel the worst about who you are, you will undoubtedly look with evil eyes on your neighbor and you will get to believe the worst about him or her." In other words, evil travels, creating a kind of domino effect: "Accuse yourself. Accuse your neighbor. Get your neighbor to accuse somebody else, and the evil spreads and thrives."[7]

Jesus Christ, by contrast, "*way* on the other side of evil," is the advocate, for Orr and for Rogers. His work is to remind and assure us "that his Father's creation is good, that we, his brothers and sisters, can look on each other as having real value. Our advocate will do anything to remind us that we are lovable and that our neighbor is lovable too!!" Orr's systematic theology began with the biblical assertion that God's creation, including humanity, is good (Gen. 1:31). Upon that foundation, Orr laid the belief that we are therefore lovable. The reconciling work of Jesus Christ includes re-minding us of our God-created goodness, and then the *good* domino effect can take off: Jesus, as advocate, reminds us that we are God's, which means we are good, which means our neighbor, who is also God's, is also good.[8] Goodness can spread and thrive too.

In 1994, Fred remembered Orr's teaching in an interview:

> My seminary professor, William Orr, who died last year, used to say something like, "Evil would want us to think the worst about who we are, so we would have that behind our eyes as we looked at our neighbor, and we would see the worst in our neighbor. Jesus would want us to see the best of who we are, so we would have that behind our eyes as we looked at our neighbor, and we would see the best in him or her. You can be an accuser or an advocate. Evil would have you be an accuser in this life. Jesus would have you be an advocate for your neighbor."
>
> That statement undergirds all of what I do through the *Neighborhood* and everything I try to do in living.[9]

If Fred's grandfather helped him to know that he was special and lovable, and if Jim Stumbaugh showed him that others could accept him just the way he was, Bill Orr taught him that the rejection of the accuser's message and the embrace of the advocate's assurance lead inevitably to the neighbor. Put another way, if we are lovable and acceptable because we are God's, then our neighbor, who is equally God's, is also lovable and acceptable. And we are called into the work of that loving and accepting.

In some ways, of course, Fred already knew this. His parents and the other community leaders in Latrobe had modeled it his whole life. You don't just take care of your own; you care for all who need care. But Orr's teaching gave that learned behavior a theological foundation, connecting the *practical* whys (because the community thrives when neighbors look out for one another, because no one can accomplish as much alone as neighbors can accomplish together) with the *theological* whys (because God has created us and called us good, because Jesus came, in part, to remind us of this essential truth).

Fred found a model of theological neighborliness in Orr. "Through all those years, I discovered that William Orr took Jesus seriously—*very* seriously! He once said to me, 'I'm betting my life on him!' And that became more and more obvious even as he suffered a stroke and lay paralyzed the last years of his life. Dr. Orr continued to teach the life of Jesus—the basis of *his* theology—even from his bed."[10] Orr believed his life had been spared for a purpose; "he was convinced like the Psalmist that his Lord had brought him out of a horrible pit and set his feet upon a rock. He was sure that he had been allowed to live so that he could act as an *advocate* for anyone who happened to be with him. What a ministry!"[11]

During those last years of Orr's life, Fred and Joanne often visited him on Sunday afternoons. Once, they were coming from church where they had sung Luther's famous hymn "A Mighty Fortress Is Our God." Fred was still mulling over one of the verses:

> And though this world, with devils filled,
> Should threaten to undo us,
> We will not fear, for God hath willed
> His truth to triumph through us:
> The prince of darkness grim,
> We tremble not for him;
> His rage we can endure,
> For lo! his doom is sure;
> One little word shall fell him.

Fred asked Dr. Orr, "What is that one little word that will fell the prince of darkness?" Bill thought for a moment, and then he replied, "One little word: *forgive*." He cited Jesus's prayer from the cross for those who persecuted and crucified him—"Father, forgive them, for they know not what they do" (Luke 23:34, ESV)—and then he continued, "You know, Fred, there's only one thing that evil cannot stand, and that is forgiveness."[12]

Though Luther scholars and hymn enthusiasts might have a different interpretation of this hymn than Orr, his read is consistent with his theology. If evil—the "prince of darkness"—is the accuser, urging us to feel bad about ourselves and our neighbors, then forgiveness brings its sure defeat. If the "rage" of "devils" comes in the form of turning us against self and neighbor, then evil's "doom" is surely in the release offered by forgiveness. And so Dr. Orr again, through example and instruction, turned Fred toward the work of neighborliness.

Later in his seminary training, Fred took a course in pastoral counseling. As part of the coursework, he was required to work as a pastoral caregiver, meeting with a "client" once a week for the whole semester. He approached the instructor and asked if he could work with a child instead of an adult. The instructor agreed on one condition: that Fred's supervisor be Margaret McFarland.

Dr. Margaret McFarland was on the faculty at the University of Pittsburgh School of Medicine, and she was also one of the founders and directors of the Arsenal Family and Children's Center, which studied child development. Dr. McFarland's colleagues and cofounders of the Arsenal Center included Dr. Benjamin Spock and Erik Erikson, and all three were at the top of their fields. Like William Orr, Margaret McFarland became much more than just an instructor to Fred

Rogers; she became a teacher in the fullest sense. He studied with her over several years at Pitt and the Arsenal Center, and they remained good friends until her death in 1988. Starting a few years after their first meeting, Margaret acted as a consultant for *Mister Rogers' Neighborhood*, and Fred met with her weekly to discuss scripts, lyrics, and the responses he received from viewers.

Margaret taught Fred innumerable lessons about child development, but the lesson from Margaret that Fred shared most often was on teaching. Once Margaret invited a sculptor from Carnegie Mellon to visit a preschool class, where Fred happened to be observing, once a week. She gave the sculptor specific instructions: "I don't want you teaching sculpting. I want you simply to sit with the children and do what you feel you'd like to do with the clay." Every time the sculptor came, she would ask him to "just love clay in front of the children."

"Well," Fred recalled, "the kids started using clay—that medium—in the most wonderful ways. And that wouldn't have happened if this gifted sculptor hadn't loved clay right in front of them."[13]

"Attitudes aren't taught," Margaret McFarland believed. "They're caught."[14]

Fred took Margaret's teaching to heart. Very practically, he made sure that his television work offered children regular opportunities to watch artists and creators of many kinds love their work in front of them—whether it be playing the cello or painting a picture or something more unexpected, like making pretzels, milking cows, or predicting the weather. He wanted children to see all sorts of people doing all sorts of things, not so they could receive step-by-step instructions on how to do the work but so they could catch the attitude of the doer and witness their love of their craft. In this way, Fred believed, children learn about the world and what they can offer it: "I mean, some child might choose painting. Some might choose playing the cello. But there are so many ways of saying who we are and how we feel, ways that don't hurt anybody."[15]

In the midst of this work, of course, Fred himself became the teacher. I think he found Margaret's lesson on teaching to be so compelling because he had experienced it: he had "caught" her attitudes, and Bill Orr's attitudes too. They loved their work in front of him, and he found it utterly convincing. Having been the beneficiary of much good teaching—from McFarland and Orr and many others too—he turned and offered himself. To put it in language like Margaret's, he loved a lot of things in front of children: music, puppetry, feelings, conversation, clarity, and people of so many sizes and shapes and colors.

And of course he loved the children themselves. I wonder if he ever considered this: that like the sculptor loving the clay in front of children, which helped them to better love the clay, he was loving *the children themselves* in front of them. Maybe he hoped they might catch that attitude too and begin to find themselves lovable like he did. Maybe this was one of his many ways of being an advocate, offering himself as Margaret and Bill offered themselves to him, in imitation of the Christ who, as Bill taught and Fred believed, wanted each person to believe the best about herself: that she was good, and lovable, and capable of loving.

8

CANADA, FATHERHOOD, AND SEPARATION

I like to be told when you're going away.

By 1962, when Fred Rogers accepted Fred Rainsberry's invitation to create a children's program for the Canadian Broadcasting Corporation (CBC), he was, so to speak, almost Mister Rogers. Strictly speaking, of course, he already was Mister Rogers (or at least Mr. Rogers), and in fact, the viewers of *The Children's Corner* knew him by name even though he rarely appeared onscreen. (Henrietta Pussycat used to speak about him regularly—"Meow, meow, meow, Mister Rogers, meow"—and Josie and Daniel Striped Tiger often referred to him by name as well.) In a deeper sense, much of what ultimately made him into the Mister Rogers that generations of Americans would love was already a part of him. But he still had to make one more crucial stop on his path to the *Neighborhood*.

Fred moved to Toronto in 1962. Joanne and their sons, Jim (born in 1959, then called Jamie) and John (born in 1961), joined him some months later, once the new Canadian show was in production.[1] They lived in Canada only until 1966,[2] but at least two enormously significant things happened there: one public and one very personal.

Fred Rogers didn't have any desire to be on camera—not even when he accepted Rainsberry's offer. In Fred's 1999 telling of the story, it wasn't until he got to Canada that he learned the details of Rainsberry's plans.

> [Rainsberry] said, "I want you to be on camera. I've seen you talk with kids."
>
> And I said, "I thought you wanted me to come and do puppets and music which is what I've always—," and he said, "No. You can do that too, but I want you to look into the lens and just pretend that that's a child. And we'll just call it *Misterogers*."
>
> I mean, talk about foresight.[3]

And so Fred Rogers stepped into the hosting role for the first time in his television career, and *Misterogers* was born. After a year of planning, the fifteen-minute program launched October 15, 1962. Most of it looked like the eventual Neighborhood of Make-Believe. (In fact, the first episodes of *Mister Rogers' Neighborhood*,[4] which debuted some years later in Pittsburgh, took their central material from the show's precursor on the CBC, adding a beginning and an end in Fred's television home to fill out a half hour.) Fred continued to develop his puppet characters, but he also had the opportunity to find his way into his own voice—Mister Rogers's voice. And he got to bring all the insights of his theological and child development coursework to bear. For the first time in his ten years in television, he was piloting his own program.

Around the time this was all happening, Fred and Joanne learned that their younger son, Johnny, who was just over a year old, needed hernia repair surgery. Even in the early '60s, this was a straightforward, outpatient procedure, and Fred and Joanne took Johnny to the hospital expecting the best. Upon checking in, they were met by a nurse and an orderly with "a crib on wheels that was like a cage," Fred recalled. The hospital staff members grabbed the sixteen-month-old boy from his parents and put him in the "crib cage." The boy screamed all the way down the hall. Fred and Joanne stood helpless and distraught in the waiting room as their son was wheeled away.

"To this day I have nightmares about it," Fred said twenty-five years later,

> and I get so angry when I talk about it that I find it hard to be the least bit charitable. If I'd known then what I know now, those people would have never taken our son from us that way. I would have insisted on being with him until he was asleep. We later learned that it took the surgical team forty-five minutes to get him sedated, and those forty-five minutes changed all of our lives.[5]

Johnny, who had been a typical, healthy toddler, emerged on the other side of surgery anxious and accident-prone. His "hernia was repaired," Fred recalled, "but his emotions were severely damaged." His ongoing emotional, behavioral, and developmental difficulties led the family to seek help for Johnny through psychotherapy, and the analyst shared with Fred that all the associations seemed to recall the experience of traumatic separation in the hospital.[6] Fred believed his son's treatment—and any medical treatment of children that disregarded their emotional and developmental needs—

was abuse in the name of medicine. He marveled, "To think that one morning in a hospital can cripple two-year-olds emotionally!"[7]

Fred didn't speak often of this trauma or its effects; privacy was always important to him and to Joanne, and they worked to keep their sons out of the limelight. But Fred did tell the hospital story publicly on at least two occasions. The first was in a speech to a group of migrant educators, in which he explained his motivation for making a television special for children facing hospital stays or surgery. The second was in a speech to the Association of Family and Conciliation Courts, addressing people whose responsibilities included the arbitration of custody disputes. Early in that speech, Fred read the Hebrew Bible story commonly known as "The Judgment of Solomon" (1 Kings 3:16–28), in which two prostitutes come to King Solomon to settle a heartrending dispute. They explain their problem: They live in the same house. They gave birth to children three days apart. And now one of the infants has died. Each woman claims that the living child is her own and the dead child is the other's, and it is up to Solomon to decide the case.

In a scheme that earned him a reputation for great wisdom, Solomon "sent for a sword, and when it was brought, he said, 'Cut the living child in two and give each woman half of it.'" At this, one of the women says, "Go on and cut it in two," while the other cries out in horror, "Please, Your Majesty, don't kill the child! Give it to her!"

And then, of course, Solomon knows which woman is the child's mother.

"This ends the reading from 1 Kings," Fred concluded—a note he had added by hand to his typed manuscript. Fred continued his speech by wondering aloud how Solomon would decide some of the cases his audience members worked on every day. "I don't need to tell you what a difficult job you have," he said. "The problem is that when we deal with a group of people—one or more of whom is a child—we just *can't* be impartial. *None* of us who have anything to do with families with young children can."[8]

I imagine his audience of lawyers, judges, educators, and counselors may have been startled by this opening, not expecting to hear Bible stories, not expecting Mister Rogers, of all people, to give *this* speech. And then Fred took them to the hospital with Johnny. And after that, through divorce and death, through loving homes and families torn apart by war.

Though the speech has the heart and clarity of any writing by Fred Rogers, its difference from the bulk of his work is striking: it is dark, threaded through with righteous anger and the regret of a haunted man. This is a father whose son was taken from his arms. This is a parent who has borne witness to the suffering of his child.

Fred Rogers—Mister Rogers—was not the same after that hospital experience. He devoted the rest of his life to issues of separation, to preventing trauma and alleviating anxiety, to honoring children and strengthening families. *Mister Rogers' Neighborhood* dealt with common childhood experiences such as hospital stays, sleepovers, and daycare. The program also addressed the separation that occurs in divorce and in death. And Mister Rogers ended each day's episode reminding children that he'd come back. Meanwhile, Fred worked with hospitals to put child- and family-centered policies in place,[9] and he connected personally with families who had experienced similar trauma.[10]

During the Gulf War, Fred wrote a letter to his good friend, the popular Senator John Heinz, after Heinz introduced a bill that would ensure that at least one parent of every young child was exempted from combat. The bill was dead on arrival, but Fred deeply appreciated his friend's efforts, writing, "We must not perpetuate abuse from one generation to the next—and separation from a young child's security (their loved ones) is a gross form of abuse."[11]

There's much about Fred Rogers's life before his son's surgery that was key to his development and to the wide ministry he undertook. But in bearing witness to his son's trauma, in feeling its fallout, he became Mister Rogers—his purpose crystallized—and he learned, in a way that even the best teachers in the most prestigious institutions of learning couldn't teach him, what was at stake in children's lives. He already believed in honoring children, treating them with respect, and taking them seriously. But now he knew firsthand, through the experience of his own child, what could be lost, even in the small, typical, day-to-day experiences of childhood. He was a witness in both senses of the word: he witnessed the trauma, as he watched and listened closely to what happened, and he also witnessed *to* the trauma, spreading the word and telling the story. Though he rarely spoke of his son's experience directly (in fact, in only one of those two speeches does he say that the young boy was his son), he built that experience—and many figurative inoculations against it—into countless narratives on *Mister Rogers' Neighborhood* and into his work in the wider world. Bearing witness, for Mister Rogers, was transformative, and in going to work to heal what he saw as largely preventable wounds, he became more himself.

9

TELEVISION AND THE CHURCH

It's the people you like the most
who can make you feel maddest.

Misterogers was a big success in Canada, but Fred and Jo-anne knew they wanted to raise their sons in the United States, near family, so in 1966, they moved back to Pittsburgh. Fred's ideas about television were now more defined and ambitious than ever. After piloting his own program with the CBC, bringing his child development knowledge and theological training to bear on his work, he knew what kind of program he wanted to create for children; *Mister Rogers' Neighborhood* was coming into focus in his imagination.

Soon after the relocation, Fred returned to WQED, hoping to bring the *Neighborhood* to fruition, but funding for the program was insecure. As he worked with local businesses and other contacts to raise support, he simultaneously began producing episodes of the new show, initially building around recordings of the fifteen-minute Canadian programs to fill out a full half hour. On November 21, 1966, *Mister Rogers' Neighborhood* began airing on the Eastern Educational Network, a regional cooperative with several member stations along the East Coast; eventually it was also picked up by stations in Los Angeles and Miami. It quickly developed an enthusiastic following, but funding was still a major concern. The *Neighborhood*'s savvy public relations team worked with local stations to plan "Meet Mister Rogers" events in Boston, Los Angeles, and other cities, and the responses were overwhelming. In one instance,

> as part of its publicity efforts to boost the program, WGBH in Boston decided to hold an open house and prepared for some 500 guests—a number they thought they would be fortunate to have. On the appointed day, WGBH was overwhelmed with more than 10,000 people—more than attended the Red Sox game that day. Shortly after that reception the Sears-Roebuck Foundation agreed to underwrite the neighborhood.[1]

Especially in the early part of his career, Fred gave a lot of thought to the church's role in television production and to television's usefulness to the church. If television could so effectively teach, connect, and resource, he reasoned, then the church should be clamoring to be a part of it.

This was also a practical matter for Fred: he needed money for his program, and as he was ordained to a ministry through media and believed he was called to "the broadcasting of grace throughout the land,"[2] he saw the church as a logical funding partner. Around the time he finished seminary in 1962, back before he went to Canada, he had made plans with the United Presbyterian Church in the United States of America to create a children's television program for the denomination, but "at the last minute the media department of the national church discovered it didn't have enough money to do any programs at all."[3] Soon after, Fred Rainsberry offered Fred Rogers the chance to develop *Misterogers* in Toronto, and he took it. But when he returned to Pittsburgh, the possibility was still in his mind: the church, he believed, could have enormous reach and impact through television and, through that, could correct much of what was potentially harmful in the medium when driven by the values of secular culture.

In 1967, an advertising executive named George Hill was acting as Fred's de facto business manager and agent as Fred searched for funding and developed his program.[4] With Hill's encouragement, Fred wrote a document titled "Children's TV: What Can the Church Do about It?" It is one of the most searing of all Fred's writings, and though it is possible that Hill, an advertiser, helped him punch up the language, the passion fueling the piece is genuine Fred Rogers:

> Do you know that children see and hear on the average of 3,000 hours of television before they ever start to school?
>
> . . . And what will they have seen and heard during these thousands of hours of watching and listening? For the major part it will have been charmingly cynic, sardonic, sadistic animated tripe with slick puns, inversions, and asides.
>
> . . . The television set is bought and placed in the home by the parents. It's as if the parents were bringing—and *condoning*—what their children see on that set. Without knowing it, are we encouraging our children to disrespect, disobey, dispel much that we feel is important in our heritage? Are our children (and the children whom the Church has never been able to reach) being fed slick stimulating sound-tracked trash 1,000 hours a year while our Church schools try to teach the

opposite with posters, crayons, and paste in one tenth the time?[5]

Fred was certainly disgusted with what children's television was often used for—demeaning treatment of others, advertising, "a steady diet of the weak always magically winning and the villains always being the big ones, of the people getting flattened out one second and popping into shape the next, of conniving and teasing and hurting and belittling and stopping tears with elaborate gifts"[6]—but he was also furious with the church. In his mind, they were not only missing an enormous opportunity but also abdicating responsibility:

> We must know this. We must know that we are failing our children; but, either we won't let ourselves admit it, or we think that there's nothing we as the Church can do about it.
>
> There *IS* something we can do! But, it's not so simple (or cheap) as writing letters of complaint! . . . We can begin to *produce* and promote television programs for children as an expression of caring for the children of the whole country. We can communicate to a child that he is accepted as he is: happy, sad, angry, lonely, *exactly* as he is.
>
> . . . The Church has given beautiful citations; but, when the question of strong financial backing comes up the Church has always had to retreat to radio jingles and spot quilt makers. . . . Let's find the money to produce, and promote long-range excellence in children's television. What a magnificent ministry it really can be![7]

It never happened, of course. Fred's fiery argument notwithstanding, the Presbyterian Church didn't fund any version of *Mister Rogers' Neighborhood*. Eva Stimson speculates in her 2000 article for the *Adventist Review* that if the Presbyterian Church had found the money to work with Fred, they "might be known today as a trailblazer in TV evangelism. On the other hand, the constraints of working within a church bureaucracy might have had a stifling effect on Rogers' creativity." And the *Neighborhood* (or its Presbyterian analogue) almost certainly would've had a smaller audience.[8]

In 1960, during their days working on *The Children's Corner*, Fred Rogers and Josie Carey filmed a special episode called "Sunday on the Children's Corner." The Presbyterian Historical Society website features the video,[9] explaining that the special is not one of the *Children's Corner* live shows but that it was probably sponsored by the Presbyterian Church and perhaps intended for home or church screenings, including use in Sunday school classes, vacation Bible schools, or the like.[10]

The thirty-minute episode maintains many of the elements of the live *Children's Corner* shows—some of the same songs, all the usual puppets and characters. The main plot arc is that some of the puppets and Josie are putting on a play. But this special episode includes many more religious elements than usual.

When Josie arrives on the Children's Corner (she gets there, as always, by thinking seventeen and a half nice thoughts in a row), Daniel Striped Tiger tells her that he was just thinking about her in Sunday school as they were singing one of his "very favorite songs." Josie and Daniel proceed to sing "Thank You for Today," a kind of prayer:

Thank you for the little things
Little things that happen every day

Thank you for those tiny things
Tiny things you surely send my way
Little things for me alone
To see, to hear, to touch
Important things I care about so much

Thank you for the smiles I see
And the ways I learn from thee each day
Thank you, God, for letting me say
I thank you gratefully
Thank you for today[11]

Then Daniel tells Josie about the play they are working on and asks her to play the part of the shoemaker's wife. He tells her that his job in this particular production is to "cheer up"; he is the official encourager—a role that he prefers to any acting role. Daniel and Josie sing "Then Your Heart Is Full of Love," a Rogers classic that stayed around in *Neighborhood* episodes until at least the mid-'90s. Though it is not explicitly religious, it contains the beautiful line "Love is fragile as your tears. Love is stronger than your fears."

Josie and Daniel continue discussing the play and sing two more songs. Then Daniel leaves to cheer up King Friday, who will be playing the shoemaker, and Josie visits with the French-speaking Grandpère. They sing a song whose lyrics are the months of the year in French, and then Josie leaves to go learn her part for the play. On her walk from Grandpère's home in the Eiffel Tower to Henrietta Pussycat's tree, she reflects on Grandpère, speaking very quickly in a blur of a monologue:

"Grandpère's so very nice. I like him so much, and I'm always surprised at how much French I'm able to learn and understand from talking with him. Reminds me of a soft thing. You know, sort of like a lamb? You know about lambs, don't you? In the Bible they're always talking about lambs. They're very important, very dear, very soft things." Then Josie sings a setting of William Blake's religious poem "The Lamb." During the song, lamb images appear onscreen—first, two illustrations that look as if they might be found in a children's book or Sunday school curriculum, and then two photos of a sculpture of a shepherd holding a lamb in his arms.

After this odd departure, the program returns its focus to the play: The characters discuss, practice, and fret about their roles. King Friday is indignant at having to play so lowly a character and insists that the audience be told they are hearing "a royal interpretation of a pedestrian dialogue." Though the part requires him to play a poor shoemaker on his last piece of leather, Friday insists that his hammer and apron be made of 14-karat gold.

When the scene fades back to Josie and X the Owl, they are, without explanation, now talking about the creation story in the Bible. They sing "Creation Duet," which asks who made the rainbow, bird, flower, and more, and then answers that God made them all. At the close of the song, X the Owl offers his theological commentary: "And you know, Jos, even though God made all this big world, and all the stars, and all the planets, the sun, and the moon, and everything, still he knows each one of us and loves us all."

"Yes, aren't we fortunate?" Josie replies.

"I know we are."

And immediately, they return to discussing their parts for the play.

Finally, it is showtime, and the production goes off with only a few hitches. King Friday is still a bit pouty about his lowly role, and the shoe leather falls down from the puppet stage to the floor a couple of times, but all in all, the play is a success.

"Sunday on the Children's Corner" closes with the song that Fred and Josie often used at the end of their Friday shows,

"Goodnight, God," a charming, earnest prayer for close of day. And Daniel offers a kind of benediction: "It's been the best Sunday, and of course we dedicate everything to our God, on Sunday and every day."

"Sunday on the Children's Corner" offers a look into what Fred Rogers might have done if he had been commissioned and funded to develop a program for the Presbyterian Church. And frankly, it doesn't look so good. The episode is sweet and humane, whimsical and creative, as all Fred's work was. But its theological portions seem shoehorned in, and the overall effect is stilted. Worse yet, the theology itself is overly simple, and it suffers from not being integrated into the rest of the plotline. The story arc of the play has real theological potential: Daniel as the encourager, each person having a role to play in the stage narrative, the wealth of King Friday and the poverty of the shoemaker. These elements and more could have been theologically mined. But instead, Fred and Josie awkwardly drop lambs and creation stories into an otherwise perfectly good *Children's Corner* narrative.

There's no doubt that Fred Rogers was creative to the core, and yet his theology—at least here—is not particularly creative. By contrast, when he is creating episodes later for the *Neighborhood*, when theology is not the stated goal, his rich and creative theology emerges naturally—but more on this in the next part.

If Fred had gotten his onetime wish of creating a program for and funded by the church, he surely would have gotten better at it. Over time, virtually every aspect of his work became more sophisticated, from puppetry to child development themes to theology. But I think it was in his best interest—and the best interest of the viewers, and perhaps even the best interest of theology—that he made a program for a wider public and not only for the church.

I think Fred was grateful, for his own reasons, in retrospect, that his pleas to the Presbyterian Church went unanswered. In 1985, radio talk-show host Terry Gross spoke to him when her program *Fresh Air* was still a local show. Gross asked him about his ordination, and he told the story of taking classes on his lunch hour, "never expecting that I would graduate. It took me eight years, and I finally graduated and was ordained a minister in the Presbyterian church."

Gross replied with a question. "Obviously you're very religious, but I don't think you . . . it's not a denominational program, and I'm sure that's intentional on your part."

"It's far from denominational and far from overtly religious," Fred said. "The last thing in the world that I would want to do would be something that's exclusive. I would hate to think that a child would feel excluded from the *Neighborhood* by something that I said and did."[12]

When the Sears-Roebuck Foundation underwrote the *Neighborhood*, Fred didn't have to worry about the future of his program anymore; his practical interest in church funding faded. Fred always believed that "you can be an agent of what's good and not have to be terribly direct about it,"[13] so he moved into *Mister Rogers' Neighborhood* and toward creative ways of living into his calling and commission. But his passion—and even his capacity for ire—didn't fade away. For the whole of his career, he believed that people working in television "are chosen to be servants to help meet deeper needs."[14] And to him, this mandate wasn't limited to those who claimed religious belief.

Fred became incensed by television programs that took advantage of children, especially through advertising. In the early days of children's television, many hosts would hawk products during their shows, incorporating a sales pitch into their activity or monologue, even going so far as to outright direct children to tell their parents what to buy on their next trip to the grocery store. Fred thought this was terrible. He worked so hard to be a trusted adult in children's lives that he simply couldn't condone using that trust to peddle a product or enrich a corporation. When WQED put his face on the side of a milk carton to sell a product, he was so upset by it that he decided to form his own nonprofit (Family Communications, Inc.) so that he would no longer be anyone's employee. He rarely approved the licensing of *Neighborhood* characters or images to be used for toys or other products (though, since his death, his company has loosened this restriction considerably).

Fred also had strong opinions about violence and chaos in children's programming. He once worked on a short-term project in the Soviet Union with a production company that wanted to create something like *Tom and Jerry*, an American cartoon with which they were familiar. "I'm sorry," Fred told them simply. "I don't like *Tom and Jerry*."[15]

Fred also took issue with programs and producers who didn't sensitively consider children's developmental needs. Though his arguments now seem a little naive, there's no doubt he held these beliefs strongly, and they informed everything he did in his own *Neighborhood*, where each line or lyric was thoroughly, painstakingly considered:

> Several years ago, I happened to be watching a television cartoon program with some children. The animation was simple yet clear. There was a deep sea diver who dove to the bottom of a lake where he found a huge plug (like a bathtub drain plug!). The diver pulled the plug loose and water started surging down the hole

at the bottom of the lake. Finally everything in the lake: the fish, the plants, the boats, the diver, EVERY-THING was sucked down the hole. Now I don't think that the creators and animators and producers of such a cartoon set out to frighten children with their work; nevertheless, any child who had any concern about being sucked down a bathroom drain (and most very young children do!) would certainly have found that cartoon horrifying. Those who created it were probably operating out of their own unresolved childhood fears; however, that is not the place from which to operate in order to create healthy productions for children. If those people (adult producers) had been well-versed in the developmental themes and needs of childhood, they would have never produced such a cartoon for preschoolers. And what's more, there wasn't even an adult on the screen at the end of the cartoon saying, "That's just pretend. Something like that could never happen . . . except in pretending. Nobody could ever get sucked down a bathroom drain."[16]

Because Fred Rogers believed that television had enormous capacity for good, he necessarily believed it had equal capacity for harm. And so, as with most everything in his life, he took it seriously and aimed to use it well.

———————

After gaining popularity over the sixteen months that it was distributed by the Eastern Educational Network, *Mister Rogers' Neighborhood* aired nationally for the first time on February 19, 1968. (Its new distributor was National Educational Television, to be replaced in 1970 by the Public Broadcasting Service, or PBS.) The music started, the camera panned over the model neighborhood and then across the porch set, the pianist played the ascending line, and the door opened. Behind it was the frightened child from the interconnected community, the awkward teen who learned that he could be liked as he was, the lonely college kid who explored his feelings through music. It was the wide-eyed twenty-something delivering coffee and Cokes to network stars, the newlywed who stopped to pray in the cathedral. It was the program manager from a fledgling station with big ideas, and the student dashing across town to get to seminary classes on time. It was the young father, standing helpless in a hospital waiting room. And it was the angry letter-writer, the striver for excellence, the man who dedicated everything, today and every day, to his God. They were all there, and they were all Mister Rogers. And he was ready.

And he walked through the door, looked into the camera, smiled, and started to sing.

BROADCASTING GRACE

Mister Rogers' Neighborhood

10

CHANGE, FEAR, AND PEACE

We all want peace.

On February 19, 1968, when *Mister Rogers' Neighborhood* airs nationally for the first time, there is trouble in the neighborhood. Lady Elaine Fairchilde, a mischief-making puppet, has rearranged the Neighborhood of Make-Believe, moving the Eiffel Tower, the factory, the fountain, and more. King Friday is unhappy about the change, and he takes out his discomfort on his subjects all week long. On Monday's episode, however, he merely expresses his displeasure, and others in the neighborhood share their own responses: X the Owl enjoys the change. Henrietta Pussycat feels shy. Daniel Striped Tiger isn't sure how to feel.

Mister Rogers, from his own house, talks about how different people respond differently to change. He points out that there have been changes made to his own home as well: new paint, a new table, a new swing on the porch.

Though this was the first national episode of *Mister Rogers' Neighborhood*, many stations—up and down the East Coast and in a few other places as well—had carried the *Neighborhood* for a year or more. Therefore, a sizable number of the program's viewers were returning, while many more were brand-new. In this first national broadcast, Fred could have written a kind of restart, introducing the program and its characters anew to his expanded public. Instead, he addressed major changes for the program, small changes in the lives of children and families, and large-scale national changes, all in a strikingly ambitious, five-day plot arc that somehow encompassed both childlike and very adult responses to change.

The changes in the Neighborhood of Make-Believe were significant (major set pieces had been moved from their locations in previous episodes) and seemingly permanent, so Fred wished to address them with his viewers; his child development training reinforced what was already his natural inclination: if you make a change that affects a child, you talk about it. In building these initial episodes around the theme of change, he also likely had in mind his cast, crew, and staff, who were themselves in the midst of great transition. The week allowed all the involved adults to process the changes to the program in their own ways.

But Fred did so much more than just name the changes. He considered how change affects people, a range of possible responses, and what consequences those responses can have. On Tuesday, in the week's second episode, we learn, along with Mister Rogers, that King Friday has established border guards in the Neighborhood of Make-Believe. When Mister Rogers tells Lady Aberlin, who is visiting his home, about the border guards, she exclaims, "Well, that sounds like a war!"

"It certainly does," Mister Rogers replies, "but at least there isn't any shooting yet."

And just like that, in the space of two episodes, a gentle acknowledgment that change affects people in different ways has evolved into the jarring possibility of war and shooting.

When the program transitions into Make-Believe, the border guard is in action. King Friday instructs Edgar Cooke that he must ask everyone—even the king's own family members—for their name, rank, and serial number. "Remember our battle cry, Edgar?" King Friday prompts. Edgar, who always speaks in song, replies, "Down with the changers, down with the changers. We don't want anything to change."

"'Cause we're on top!" King Friday exclaims.

"That's right," Edgar sings, though he sounds less enthused about it than Friday. "'Cause we're—at least you're—on top."

King Friday, satisfied, goes back inside the castle. Then Lady Aberlin, the king's niece, comes by for a visit, unwittingly putting Edgar's new training to the test. After some confusion about serial numbers and ranks, Edgar is satisfied and goes to request an audience with the king on her behalf. "This is strange!" Lady Aberlin marvels when Edgar leaves. "I used to be able to walk right in here."

The consequences are piling up: Lady Aberlin cannot see her own uncle without submitting (and first creating) her serial number; Henrietta, the audience learns, is very frightened and won't leave her home; X the Owl suggests that war is on the way. And when Lady Aberlin is granted time with the king, she learns that she is not allowed to joke anymore, and she is allowed to sing a song only if none of the words have changed. She also asks about the stars she notices on Edgar's and the king's military helmets. The king's helmet has thirteen stars on it, while Edgar's has only one. "Edgar is only a one-star man," Friday explains. "I am a thirteen-star king!"

At the end of the segment, King Friday drafts Lady Aberlin into his border guard. She doesn't want to join, but she is conscripted: he gives her a uniform, runs her through training drills, and assigns her a post. So far, fear of change has led to reduced mobility, open suspicion, frightened civilians, and an outfitted, ranked military with a draft.

Michael G. Long's book, *Peaceful Neighbor*, provides important context for this first week of national programs:

> Just three weeks before the national launch of *Mister Rogers' Neighborhood* in February 1968, Ho Chi Minh and his advisers in North Vietnam marked Tet, the Vietnamese lunar New Year, by carrying out a surprise assault on cities and villages across South Vietnam. The Tet Offensive was massive, with 84,000 pro-Communist troops staging attacks throughout the South, and although U.S. and South Vietnamese forces took just several days to repel the attackers, the sheer power of the assault suggested that President Johnson and General Westmoreland had been less than forthcoming in their earlier assurances that the Vietnam conflict was near its end.
>
> Frustration at home was palpable. "What the hell is going on?" CBS news anchor Walter Cronkite angrily asked. "I thought we were winning the war!" . . .
>
> Although only a small minority of citizens were antiwar activists, protests were on the rise, and just two weeks before *Mister Rogers' Neighborhood* debuted nationally, Martin Luther King Jr. had led 2,500 members of a major antiwar group, Clergy and Laity Concerned about Vietnam, in a silent vigil at Arlington National Cemetery.[1]

While King Friday was calling for border guards, Mister Rogers's viewers were living in a nation steeped in war. "Major media outlets had been bringing home the horrors of war by offering daily doses of violent images and death counts."[2] Children, Fred knew, were seeing some of these news reports, hearing the adults in their lives talk about the war, and sensing even unspoken tensions. So his ambitious first week of programming addressed this national turmoil as well. By showing some of the consequences of living in an atmosphere of political tensions, Mister Rogers provided children with tools for their own processing and understanding.

The third episode of the week contains a particularly moving subplot. On Wednesday, Chef Brockett comes to visit Mister Rogers, and together, they make a cake for the king. The process of measuring and mixing, baking and icing, takes nearly seven minutes onscreen, a quarter of the episode; its importance is clear. When the chef arrives in the Neighborhood of Make-Believe with the cake, he cheerfully gives his name, rank (master chef), and serial number (1234567). He presents the cake, and the king asks Lady Aberlin to cut a piece. She does, but when she offers it to the king, he asks for another. Assuming he wants a larger piece—"king-size!"—Lady Aberlin cuts a more generous helping and offers the cake again.

"Another piece, please," the king says, and Chef Brockett is delighted; the king must think it looks wonderful to ask for so many pieces. As Lady Aberlin offers the king a third slice—this one a full quarter of the cake—the king says, "One more," and then asks what is in the cake. Chef Brockett begins to list the ingredients, but King Friday interrupts: "Yes, I realize that, but I am wondering if there are any secret messages of *change* within," and he spits out the word *change* with disgust.

Lady Aberlin's face falls. Chef Brockett assures the king he would never hide a secret message of change inside a cake. But King Friday urges Lady Aberlin to cut "another piece, and another piece," and she and the chef both become distraught as she continues to cut through the cake, which now begins to fall apart. The chef puts his hands on his head and cries, "Oh, my poor cake!"

King Friday, unmoved, asks again, "Are there any messages of change in there?"

"No!" Lady Aberlin replies. "Do you want to look?" And as she brings the cake over to show the king, its instability is obvious: a piece of it falls to the ground.

"I not only want to look," the king says. "I want to *smell* to see if there are any poisonous materials in there."

Chef Brockett is offended and hurt, and Lady Aberlin is also very upset. The king sniffs the cake, proclaims it fine to eat, and gives the troops permission to do so. But he goes inside without eating any, offering only a perfunctory thank-you to the chef. When Lady Aberlin offers a piece to Edgar, he is wary, and when she offers some to Chef Brockett, he also declines. "No, thank you," he says. "I don't feel like eating anything right now."

The scene is about as devastating as *Mister Rogers' Neighborhood* ever gets. Where Tuesday's episode laid out a range of responses to change, Wednesday's showed that those responses have real, human consequences. Change causes fear, in some people if not all—this is a surety. But fear, if allowed to run rampant, can destroy creativity, rob pleasure from others, and deeply wound those in our care: the chef's heartfelt offering ends up on the ground.

Wednesday's emotional rifts become visible and tangible on Thursday: Overnight, a barbed-wire fence has been erected between the castle and the rest of the Neighborhood of Make-Believe. At the king's orders, Handyman Negri installs punch clocks on every neighborhood structure. Everyone is required to punch in and punch out, logging their movements whenever they travel around the neighborhood. By the end of the episode, even Mister Rogers punches a clock at his home before leaving for the day. It has taken only four days for King Friday's fear to create walls and constraints in all of their lives. Interestingly, King Friday himself does not appear in this episode. No matter; his influence is felt everywhere.

By Friday, Lady Aberlin and Daniel Striped Tiger have hatched a plan. They started plotting because, as Lady Aberlin tells Mister Rogers, "he asked me, Didn't I think we could do something about all that separation?" So overnight, they wrote messages—"peaceful coexistence," "love," "tenderness," and "peace"—on tags, which they attach to balloons. They plan to float the balloons to the castle to try to change King Friday's mind.

After Mister Rogers rehearses the plan with Lady Aberlin and wishes her the best, the program transitions to Make-Believe to find King Friday instructing Edgar and Handyman Negri: "Any trouble, fire the shot. We shall meet here for further instructions." After the king returns to the castle, Handyman Negri asks, "Edgar, what do you think he means by 'any trouble'?"

"Well, he probably means that he's still afraid someone will make more changes," Edgar replies. "What a week it's been. And so many people have had their feelings hurt."

When Lady Aberlin and Daniel launch their plan—and the balloons—things almost go all wrong: King Friday comes out shouting, "Fire the cannon! Fire the cannon! Man your stations, everybody!"

"What is it, King Friday?" asks Handyman Negri.

"Paratroopers!"

Lady Aberlin and Handyman Negri help King Friday to see that there are messages attached to the balloons. When he reads them, he is converted: "Stop all fighting!" he says. "Oh, what a surprise."

Lady Elaine Fairchilde, who made the changes to the neighborhood that so unsettled Friday, shows up for the first time all week to find out what all the excitement is about. King Friday tells her it is her fault, and she is characteristically delighted. The king and Lady Elaine retreat into the castle to talk, and when they leave, Lady Aberlin, Daniel, X, and Handyman Negri begin to take down the barbed wire, joyful and relieved that their plan worked.

Back in Mister Rogers's house, he sums up the week in his candid Mister Rogers way: "Isn't peace wonderful?"

———————

Michael G. Long makes a compelling case that Fred Rogers was a "dyed-in-the-wool pacifist who saw war and its preparations as always wrong."[3] It does seem clear that this opening week of programming was responding to war abroad and to tensions about war at home. But Fred also cared very much about a root cause of so many conflicts: change and the fear of it. And he saw it everywhere—from the daily changes that children deal with, like new siblings or new houses or new routines, to the changes his staff was navigating as their program reached new audiences, to the changes of a country in increasing turmoil. As always, Fred cared about what was happening on the insides of people as they met those changes with joy, curiosity, fear, or uncertainty. And as always, he cared what people did with those feelings, because behaviors have consequences to individuals, to their neighbors, and to their neighborhoods—of whatever size they may be.

When Fred Rogers made programs about war (which he would do again in the '80s—see chapter 12), or when he addressed issues of difference (which he did from his first show to his very last), he wasn't addressing only those grown-up needs like armed conflict or integration. He was connecting the dots, as he was remarkably good at doing, between the grown-up versions of these social realities and their analogue issues in childhood. If we are going to meaningfully address war, he believed, we must address children's fear of the changes in their own lives. If we are going to work on our own fears of political change and military escalation, we must work on how children feel when the kitchen table is different and the walls have been painted.

If we are going to develop generations of emotionally intelligent adults, we must address the emotional needs of the children who will become them.

———————

The last thing Mister Rogers offered in his first week of national *Neighborhood* episodes was a prayer. "We have a song at our house," he says by way of introduction. "Not everybody sings this song, but we do." And he sings,

> Goodnight, God, and thank you for this very lovely day.
> Thank you, too, for keeping us at work and at our play.
> Thank you for our families. For each and every friend.
> Forgive us, please, for anything we've done that might
>   offend.
>
> Keep us safe and faithful, God. Tell us what to do.
> Goodnight, God. And thank you, God, for letting us love
>   you.
> Goodnight, God. And thank you, God, for letting us love
>   you.[4]

He sang this song, probably, because it was Friday, and he and Josie Carey often sang it at the end of their Friday episodes of *The Children's Corner* many years before. But Fred's choice to sing "Goodnight, God" at the end of *this* week reveals something about how his theology impacted his work in the wider world. Quite simply, his theological conviction sat comfortably alongside all the work he felt called into: the work of helping children develop well, the work of doing justice in a frightened, angry, hurting world. His "lovely days" were filled with "work" and "play" that he dedicated, at day's end, to God. And all of it, for Fred, was an expression of love for the God he believed would see him through until morning, when he'd get up and do it all again.

11

NEIGHBORHOOD LITURGY

I'll be back when the day is new.

Children are creatures of liturgy. For that matter, so are adults. We humans respond very well to routine. Some of us crave or even require it. Inarguably, we are shaped by it; whatever we do again and again, in the same order, in the same kinds of ways, conditions us to expect whatever comes next. When the music starts, we expect it to finish. When the piano begins its ascending line, we know, by the time we reach the top, we'll see Mister Rogers opening the door.

Freddy Rogers spent every Sunday of his childhood at Latrobe Presbyterian Church. He squirmed in the pews, got shushed by his parents, no doubt left mid-service sometimes to go to the bathroom. During long sermons he studied the stained glass windows, with their depictions of lilies, holly, and rose of Sharon, or gazed up at the broad, round light fixtures, gold leaves and flowers circling their edges. As he got older, he participated more and more: standing to sing or recite creeds, shaking hands during the passing of the peace, receiving the bread and wine during Communion. Even as Fred grew, these rituals didn't necessarily convey great meaning each and every Sunday; like all of us, Fred sometimes just went through the motions. But then, that's what liturgy is all about: we go through the motions, again and again, because we believe those motions make us who we are. Those rituals—to use language that Fred Rogers might use—help us to grow on the inside.

Fred Rogers was probably the rare college kid who kept on going to church even when he left home. After college, when he moved to New York, he sought out moments of prayer in St. Patrick's Cathedral, and when he saw Joanne Byrd in person for the first time after proposing to her by mail, he asked her to take him to the church where she sang in the choir on Sundays. It was there, in a church pew, that he gave her a diamond ring and they shared a kiss.[1] Later, during the months when Fred and Josie Carey were flying to New York City each weekend to air NBC's weekly episode of *The Children's Corner*, Fred insisted on flying back to Pittsburgh on Saturday nights so he could be home for church on Sundays. The Rogers family's liturgy of attending church, and the church's own liturgies of word and sacrament, did exactly what they were supposed to do: they formed Fred Rogers into the kind of person who keeps the liturgy.

So it's no wonder that when Fred designed his own program in his own neighborhood, he built both out of liturgies: the music accompanying the aerial shot of the (model) neighborhood, the musical ascent coinciding with the camera's approach to the house, the opening door, the singular man. Next: the song, the blazer off and onto the hanger, the sweater on and zipped, the loafers traded for sneakers. And the greeting: "Hello, neighbor!"

Here, the format loosened, but the liturgies didn't end. For instance, Mister Rogers always told his television neighbors about where they were going and what they would be doing before any of it happened. The trolley always led into the Neighborhood of Make-Believe. At some point in each episode, Mister Rogers fed his fish.

> In a sense, Rogers' "television house," as he calls it, is a children's church, and the program . . . is a children's service, with its own rituals (the donning of the sneakers and cardigan sweater, the feeding of the fish), readings (from the gospel of King Friday from the Neighborhood of Make-Believe), hymns (the many Neighborhood songs he composes), and sermons (the show's "important talk," about, say, the death of a goldfish).[2]

Like all good liturgies, Mister Rogers's liturgies were open to growth and change. Famously, he received a letter from a child who was blind, saying she worried sometimes about whether he had fed the fish. From then on, he always spoke aloud that he was giving the fish their food.[3] He also simplified his transitions to and from Make-Believe (early episodes had a two-part transition, including a telescope as well as a trolley, and sometimes a pull-out couch or a tin-can telephone). And his closing song changed from "Tomorrow" in the early days to "It's Such a Good Feeling," to which, still later, he added the tag that begins, "I'll be back when the day is new . . ." assuring that the liturgy would return again.

Some of the elements of the liturgy originated in practicality. For instance, Fred began wearing tennis shoes during the days of *The Children's Corner* because he frequently had to run from the organ, which sat at the far end of the studio, to the main set. Quite simply, he needed shoes that enabled him to run quietly. Later, the shoes took on a different significance, cuing children that their time together would be comfortable and casual, and, just as importantly, that it would be set apart from the rest of the more buttoned-up workday. (Incidentally, "set apart" is the Sunday school–approved definition of the word *holy*. It's no stretch at all to say that Fred believed his visits with his television neighbors to be times of holy exchange.)

Fred thought very carefully about the elements of his program, and virtually everything was done with intention. Each episode progresses from left to right "to accustom the children's eyes to reading."

> Each scene begins with a wide setup shot; the disembodied heads of extreme closeups are avoided to preserve what psychologists call "body integrity"; and comings and goings are always elaborately staged. The neighbors rarely appear without telephoning first, then are greeted extravagantly when they arrive. And no one leaves without saying goodbye. Topics come and go in the same deliberate way—introduced, explained, restated, and finally dismissed.[4]

This intentionality came from all the most important parts of who Fred was. It was clearly due in large part to his child development training, which taught him about children's reliance on routine. In 1991, as the Gulf War was beginning, Fred Rogers's nonprofit, Family Communications, sent a memo to PBS stations across the country. "As the adult world with its Persian Gulf situation continues to provide uncertainty and distress, we in Public Television can help young children by providing their regular and predictable preschool programming," the memo said. "Knowing what to do comforts preschoolers."[5]

The consistent format and elements of the program, and the way those elements worked together, were also connected

to Fred's musical training. Fred often explained the relationship between the program segments in his television home
and the segments in Make-Believe using the musical metaphor of theme and variation.[6] "He likens a transition to the
modulation between two keys," John Sedgwick wrote in his
1989 profile of Fred. "You always want to work with the three
or four or five common notes for a while before you get from
one to the other," Fred told him.[7]

But I suspect that the deepest reason for the program's shape
was that Fred was a person formed in liturgy. When he returned
to a song about fear or anger or love that he had sung dozens of
times before, it was partly because his child development training told him that children thrive on routine. It was partly because his musical training taught him how a melody can anchor
learning in abiding memory. But it was mostly because, somewhere in the oldest parts of himself, Fred remembered standing
to sing "A Mighty Fortress Is Our God" on Sundays when he felt
sad or scared—or, for that matter, content or bored. He remembered the relief of standing, after a long sermon, and taking a
deep breath. He remembered his mother's voice above and to
one side, and his father's voice above and to the other, the way
their voices rose and converged, how his own young voice found
the melody by fitting itself into his parents' larger, surer voices
like a hand into a glove. He remembered how he believed a little
better when he sang, and how he carried the melody through
the day, whether he meant to or not.

———————

The grown-up Fred Rogers, in his life away from the *Neighborhood*, was a man of liturgy as well. He rose early each morning
to read his Bible and to pray, and then he went to the pool for a
swim before heading to work. "Years ago," he told his viewers
during a 1982 episode of *Mister Rogers' Neighborhood*, "I promised

myself that I would try to swim a certain length of time each day. And I've done that almost every day for more than ten years."[8] Fred shared, in the spring of 2000, that he was in the practice of standing on the side of the pool, before beginning his swim, and singing "Jubilate Deo," a song from the Taizé community in France. The song's words, "Jubilate Deo," mean simply "Rejoice in God." "I don't sing it very loud," he added.[9]

Fred's swimming liturgy led to another one, one that is practically cellular and not a little strange. Tom Junod's profile tells it best:

> Mister Rogers weighed 143 pounds because he has weighed 143 pounds as long as he has been Mister Rogers, because once upon a time, around thirty-one years ago, Mister Rogers stepped on a scale, and the scale told him that Mister Rogers weighs 143 pounds. No, not that he *weighed* 143 pounds, but that he *weighs* 143 pounds. And so, every day, Mister Rogers refuses to do anything that would make his weight change—he neither drinks, nor smokes, nor eats flesh of any kind, nor goes to bed late at night, nor sleeps late in the morning, nor even watches television—and every morning, when he swims, he steps on a scale in his bathing suit and his bathing cap and his goggles, and the scale tells him that he weighs 143 pounds. This has happened so many times that Mister Rogers has come to see that number as a gift, as a destiny fulfilled, because, as he says, "the number 143 means 'I love you.' It takes one letter to say 'I' and four letters to say 'love' and three letters to say 'you.' One hundred and forty-three. 'I love you.' Isn't that wonderful?"[10]

When Fred traveled to different time zones, he didn't change his watch, his schedule, or his routine. Bill Isler, president and CEO of Family Communications (later the Fred Rogers Company) from 1987 until 2016, remembers Fred once calling his hotel room in California at 4 a.m. Fred asked Bill if he wanted to go to the gym and run while Fred was swimming. Bill declined; Fred was unfazed.[11] Fred also made a point, wherever he was, to play the piano every day.

Fred's discipline and intentionality showed up even in his everyday speech. *Mister Rogers' Neighborhood* was a "program" and never a "show." Children and families "used" rather than "watched" the program; they were not merely passive receivers, and his language acknowledged their agency and activity. Fred avoided the first person, when he could, and he especially avoided the possessive pronoun *my*. Instead he spoke of "our work" or "our offices" when speaking of his professional life, and when referring to his home life, he always referred to "our sons," "our home," or "our family."

I asked several people what they made of Fred's remarkable discipline. Was it something he craved or even required? Or was it something he worked at even if it didn't come naturally? Bill Isler credited the influence of Fred's parents: his businessman father and service-oriented mother were both people of discipline. He also pointed to Fred's musical life. "I remember sitting on a front porch one time, and a young woman across the street was practicing piano," Bill told me. "And I said, 'I could listen to that all the time. It's just a lot of fun.'" Fred replied, "It's not any fun for her." Bill also remembers Fred sharing the wisdom of Christoph von Dohnányi, Fred and Joanne's friend from Rollins who became a famous conductor. He would say, "If I miss one practice, I know. If I miss two practices, the conductor knows. If I miss three practices, the audience knows." On the program, Bill reminded me, Fred would emphasize both talent and hard work whenever he brought an artist or athlete to meet his television neighbors. "Yeah," Bill said, "discipline is something he worked at."[12]

Fred worked hard to be a disciplined person because it was of paramount importance to him that he be a trustworthy adult. As noted in chapter 9, Fred believed that people who worked in television were entrusted with enormous responsibility, and he worked to be worthy of what he believed was a high calling. On the *Neighborhood*, this translated in ways both broad and specific: Broadly, he strove to be exactly the same person on screen as off. Specifically, he made small changes over time to move toward consistency and honesty. The lines between reality and Make-Believe in early episodes were blurry—King Friday even spoke to Mister Rogers by phone—but later, the boundaries were absolute. When Big Bird was to appear on *Mister Rogers' Neighborhood*, Fred requested that he be able to show his audience how the puppet was operated and to introduce Caroll Spinney, the puppeteer, to his viewers. When Spinney declined, Fred insisted that Big Bird appear only in the Neighborhood of Make-Believe, where anything is possible. To have Big Bird visit Mister Rogers's television home as a character would have been, in Fred's worldview, dishonest.[13]

Fred cultivated honesty and consistency in himself the same way he cultivated love of self in his viewers: by choosing good liturgies and keeping them day after day, program after program, prayer after prayer, and song after song.

———————

Less than a year before Fred died, his friend Tim Madigan, a journalist, asked him to share his favorite poem for a newspaper article. Fred replied, at length, in an email that revealed the staying power of his liturgies:

> Those lines which we read, and sometimes memorize,
> at the beginning of our lives travel with us all our

days. . . . And so I must admit there is a "favorite" poem from every poet I have ever loved. But to choose one favorite I find myself going even further back in my life to a psalm of King David, which my parents recited to me many, many times when I was very, very young.

"The Lord is my Shepherd, I shall not want. He maketh me to lie down in green pastures . . . "

I can hear both my mother's and my father's voices saying that psalm. . . . Throughout my life, I've studied that psalm—that song, that poem—in different English translations as well as in different languages and have read countless scholarly commentaries, and while I have long since given up the "thees" and "thous" of most biblical translations, the Psalm 23 that I repeat every day is the one my parents "taught" me all those years ago. In 1970, when my Dad was very ill and I had to go on a two-day work trip I remember as vividly as if it were only yesterday the last things we talked about . . . and right after that we just naturally said the 23rd Psalm together. The next day, while I was away, Dad died. "I will dwell in the house of the Lord forever" are the last words we spoke with each other in this life.[14]

The word *liturgy* comes from the Greek *leitourgia*, often translated as "the work of the people." Shaped as he was by liturgy, Fred quietly ushered his viewers—and even his staff—into that work too, through songs and shoes and goldfish, and even the piano theme from 1940s Pathé newsreels that he played to signal that the filming day was done.[15] Through his liturgies, Mister Rogers discipled millions of people into the work—the hard, sometimes monotonous, always soul-expanding work—of neighborly love.

12

PARABLES OF THE KINGDOM

Won't you be my neighbor?

Fred Rogers found his own faith, at times, a little uncomfortable to talk about. "I think it's really tough—for some people, it's very easy to talk about spiritual things, and I get really turned off by those who can be so glib about it," he said. Fred came from a reticent, practical family, dedicated to faith and service without ever wanting to broadcast either one. He also worried, at times, about the potential impact on his program or his viewers if he talked about his beliefs too openly: "This is all very personal, you know. I have never flaunted my faith. In fact, there were years when I wouldn't tell people about my ordination because I didn't want anybody to think that I was using it in any way to further the program in the eyes of certain groups.

"And, I also didn't want some children to feel excluded."

Still, Fred knew that his faith infused his work. "I think that my faith has affected everything that I've done," he said, "but that's only natural; so have my genes."[1] Whether he was vocal about it or not, faith was as fundamental to Fred as DNA.

To bridge the gap between his discomfort and caution on the one side and the faith that made him who he was on the other, he relied on story. "What a tough job to try to communicate the gift of Jesus Christ to anybody," he marveled in a 1979 letter to a friend. "It can't be simply talked about, can it? Jesus himself used parables—so I guess that's our directive: try to show the kingdom of God through stories as much as possible."[2]

Christians of many stripes find plenty to argue about when it comes to what "the kingdom of God" entails. Most agree that it's not simply heaven, some other place in some other realm. Rather, it has to do with the establishment of God's order on earth, both now, in a way that is ongoing and ever-becoming, and in the future, in a more definite, final, full form. "God's order" looks something like the vision offered by the words of Isaiah that Jesus reads in the temple at the start of his ministry: good news for the poor, release for prisoners, sight for the blind, and liberation for the oppressed. This, Isaiah writes and Jesus reads, is what God's favor looks like (Luke 4:18–19).

But Jesus had trouble talking about the kingdom of God too. As Fred notes in his letter, Jesus most often tried to explain God's kingdom through parables, many of which begin, "The kingdom of God is like . . ." He tries again and again, throughout the Gospels, to find an apt metaphor, even asking aloud, "What is God's kingdom like? To what can I compare it?" (Luke 13:18, CEB; see also Luke 13:20 and Mark 4:30). It's almost as if each attempt leaves him dissatisfied, and so he tries one more time.

Fred patterned his own storytelling after this example. The Neighborhood of Make-Believe, with its eclectic cast of puppets and people, was the perfect place for Fred to stage his own parables and work out his own theology of the kingdom of God. Though many of his storylines were theological only in the loosest sense, some showed his kingdom theology clearly. A striking example is the narrative arc during a week on conflict (episodes 1521–25), which first aired in November 1983.

Since *Mister Rogers' Neighborhood*'s first national week in 1968, a lot had changed. King Friday had married Queen Sara Saturday in 1969, and Prince Tuesday was born in 1970. In the wider world, the Vietnam War receded, coming to a definitive end in 1975, but new political tensions were mounting as, in the early '80s, the anticommunist Reagan administration intervened in Central America and the Caribbean islands. At the same time, the United States, along with much of the developed world, was pursuing ever-increasing nuclear power.[3] Fred was as concerned as ever about war and its myriad costs, so he crafted a parable for his Neighborhood of Make-Believe to represent a better way—a kingdom of God, "gift of Jesus Christ" kind of way.

Prince Tuesday's class at the neighborhood school is in the middle of a social studies lesson, studying a world map, when they have occasion to remember that part of Side-Step Land used to be called Down-Under Land before their recent war. "We've never had a war here in Make-Believe, have we?" the prince asks. "Not that I know of," Miss Cow replies. "There's no mention of a war in this neighborhood in any of the history books."

Later in the day, the prince arrives home and confirms with his father that it's true: there have been no wars in Make-Believe. But that may be about to change. King Friday has just learned about neighboring Southwood's order of "parts" from Cornflake S. Pecially's factory in the Neighborhood of Make-Believe. King Friday, who did not entirely resign his fears (and consequent warring tendencies) after receiving those peace balloons in 1968, immediately suspects that Southwood must be planning to build bombs. In the week's second episode, he finds out just how many parts Southwood has ordered—one million!—and this, to him, confirms his suspicion. In response, he places his own order with Corney's factory: "If Southwood has a million, we will have a million and one!"

Tensions build within the Neighborhood of Make-Believe over the course of the week. Thanks to a healthy neighborhood bank balance, King Friday has recently convened a committee to recommend a purchase for the neighborhood school. Lady Elaine, a committee member, has decided to recommend the purchase of a record player, but then she learns that the money will be going instead to the factory to pay for the million and one parts. As the parts begin to be delivered, King Friday puts Make-Believe residents to work building bombs in the castle. Finally, on the week's fourth episode, Lady Aberlin and Lady Elaine, the neighborhood dissidents, form a peace delegation and travel to Southwood to investigate. Upon arriving, they discover the real reason for Southwood's order: they aren't building bombs after all; they're building a bridge.

The residents of Make-Believe—King Friday included—are relieved to learn that Southwood's intentions are peaceful. They plan a celebration with their new friends, and King Friday apologizes. The kind bridge builder from Southwood even uses some of the parts King Friday purchased in his warmongering fear to build the record player the neighborhood can no longer afford. The king, once again converted, pledges to build record players from the rest of the million and one parts, and to give one to every school in the world.

As Mister Rogers is leaving his television house at the end of the week's final episode, he pauses on his porch to sing:

> Peace and quiet.
> Peace, peace, peace.
> Peace and quiet.
> Peace, peace, peace.
>
> Peace and quiet.
> Peace, peace, peace.
> We all want peace;
> We all want peace.[4]

Following the song, as Mister Rogers leaves for the weekend, the screen fades to a shot of these words:

> And they shall beat their swords into plowshares,
> And their spears into pruning forks;
> Nation shall not lift up sword against nation,
> Neither shall they learn war any more.

The quote is unattributed—Fred was still hesitant about broadcasting his beliefs so overtly, a hesitation that seems ironic after the week's bold storyline—but it comes from Isaiah 2:4, in which the prophet recounts his vision of God's good future, the kingdom of God, realized at last on the earth.

It's almost as if Fred Rogers began the week saying, "The kingdom of God is like . . ." and filled in the rest with a story. For Fred, if the kingdom of God is a place where swords are beaten into plowshares, then it is a place where bombs are built into bridges, where the wasteful accumulations of fear and power are converted into record players, where children's needs—once sacrificed to the warring whims of kings—are ultimately met, where even the warring king can be converted through connection. The kingdom of God, for Fred Rogers, is a neighborhood.

Perhaps the neighborhood, and the idea of neighboring, was Mister Rogers's most persistent parable—if also his most covert. "Hello, neighbor," "I'd like you to know my television neighbor," "It's a beautiful day in this neighborhood," "the Neighborhood of Make-Believe"—the "neighbor" language is so omnipresent, it's easy to miss how theological it is. Mister Rogers, who carefully considered every word he spoke on-screen, didn't call his viewers "acquaintances" or "friends"; he didn't call us "boys and girls" or "ladies and gentlemen." He called us "neighbors."

There's no denying that "neighbor" is biblical language. The Hebrew Bible instructs God's people to "love your neighbor as yourself" (Lev. 19:18, CEB), and in the New Testament, Jesus discusses this commandment with a legal expert who tries to lay a conversational trap for him (Luke 10:25–37, CEB).

"And who is my neighbor?" the scholar asks slyly.

And Jesus answers, as he often did, and as Fred Rogers himself learned to do, with a story. In the story, a man is beaten by thieves and left to die. A priest—a powerful man, both religiously and politically—approaches, sees the injured man, and crosses to the other side of the road to avoid helping. Then another religious leader does the same. Finally, someone else comes down the road, someone of the wrong class or the wrong color, a member of a despised group. Though he is on a journey, he stops. "Moved with compassion," he tends the injured man, takes him to an inn, and pays for his lodging and care.

"What do you think?" Jesus asks his tricky interlocutor after finishing the story. "Which one of these three was a neighbor?"

And though perhaps he can't believe he is saying so, the scholar answers, "The one who demonstrated mercy toward him."

When Mister Rogers called his viewers "neighbors," when he hosted us in his neighborhood for over thirty years, he was playing out his own greatest parable: calling us, gently but firmly, into lives of mercy and care for one another. He knew we wouldn't always get it right, that we are prone, like the king he lovingly created, to bow to fear and to serve competition, to privilege our own safety and to neglect others' real needs. Maybe, in calling us neighbors, he knew he was calling us something better than we actually were. But maybe he believed that if he got to us while we were young, if he told us, again and again, that we are good, that we are lovable, and that we can build bridges of mercy, maybe we could grow into real neighbors to one another.

13

DIFFERENCE IN THE
NEIGHBORHOOD

I like someone who sings like, and walks like,
and talks like, and looks like you.

Fred Rogers was ahead of his time on issues of difference and diversity.[1] From the very first week of his program, during which an African American teacher brings an inter-racial group of her students to sing songs around Mister Rogers's kitchen table, he made it clear: his *Neighborhood*, and the Neighborhood of Make-Believe within it, are places where people are not all the same. This was both a radical statement and a patently banal one: it is radical to affirm difference in a world so terrified of change (and fear of change, remember, was at the heart of week one's narrative); but for Fred, difference is not a disruption or a departure but simple reality. Difference is an integral part of any neighborhood, and Mister Rogers's casual yet persistent presentation of it was meant less to highlight and more to normalize.

By the summer of 1968, François Clemmons was a regular character on *Mister Rogers' Neighborhood*. An African American opera singer, François played one of the first recurring African American characters on a children's television program. He was initially uncomfortable being cast as a police officer: "I grew up in the ghetto, and I did not have a positive opinion of police officers," Clemmons reflected.[2] But Fred's vision prevailed, as it usually did.

One of the most famous moments in *Mister Rogers' Neighborhood* history came in the spring of 1969. In episode 1065, Mister Rogers fills a baby pool in the yard of his television house and invites Officer Clemmons to stop for a moment and soak his feet. Clemmons hesitates since he doesn't have a towel, but Mister Rogers simply says, "Oh, you share mine." The two men sit side by side, and the camera zooms in to show Clemmons's brown feet next to Mister Rogers's pale ones. Though this image would be meaningful at any time, it arose in a particular historical context: In 1969, plenty of places in the South (and not-so-South) were still struggling to integrate. Just five years earlier, on June 18, 1964, black and white protesters jumped into the whites-only pool at the Monson Motor Lodge in St. Augustine, Florida. In retaliation, the owner of the hotel poured acid into the pool. Many people believe that the horrific television footage from the Monson Motor Lodge contributed to the passage, the very next day, of the Civil Rights Act,[3] following a sixty-day filibuster in the US Senate. Still, this monumental victory by no means ended the struggle: Just three days later, protesters in St. Augustine held a similar wade-in at a "whites only" public beach. They were met by "an angry gang of whites [who] used their fists and clubs to assault the interracial group . . . , sending more than a handful to the hospital."[4] None of this was far in the national rear view when Mister Rogers and Officer Clemmons rested their feet in the water for the nation to see. For Mister Rogers, this was a normal day in the neighborhood. Commenting on the heat of the day, he says, "Sometimes just a minute like this will really make a difference."

Fred Rogers also dealt deftly—especially for his time—with issues of gender on the *Neighborhood*. He often did tasks that many of his viewers might have considered "feminine," such as diapering a baby doll, washing dishes, ironing, caretaking, and knitting.[5] And he used his Neighborhood of Make-Believe to show an even wider range of gender roles and expressions. Lady Elaine, for instance, is a mischief-maker as well as an entrepreneur, running a museum, traveling to space, and anchoring a news program. She even says, in episode 1068 from 1970, "I'm tired of being a lady!" Mayor Maggie, who appeared first on the program in 1975, is the African American mayor of Westwood, which, as Long points out in *Peaceful Neighbor*, makes her King Friday's political and social equal. Arguably, Fred's entire program was built on a gender-bending premise:

> Just the thought of a middle-aged man coming into a child's home in the middle of the day was countercultural in the 1960s. Most adult males were absent from their homes at that point; they were at work, talking about adult things with other adults. But there was Mister Rogers, taking time before his own workday, or so he told us, to come to his television house and spend thirty minutes of quality time with boys and girls across the nation.[6]

In a neighborhood, the program quietly yet insistently asserts, there are many ways to be boys and men, girls and women.

Mister Rogers' Neighborhood shows awareness of socioeconomic difference too. In 1972, Fred crafted a storyline in Make-Believe about a financially struggling magician concerned about providing his family with the clothes and food they need. From his television home, Mister Rogers uses the opportunity to speak with children about how sometimes parents can't afford to buy everything they'd like for their children.

He even builds a pointed message into the Make-Believe narrative, when King Friday doubts the magician's need because he doesn't look poor. When he finds out later that the magician has sold his cape in order to buy breakfast for his hungry family, the king is appalled. Always the model of conversion, he proceeds to form a foundation to help care for artists in need.[7] Awareness of socioeconomic difference is also promoted on the program through Queen Sara Saturday, who is the Neighborhood of Make-Believe's connection to global hunger: she works with an organization called Food for the World, even taking on the job full-time in a 1989 storyline.[8] Financial need, in *Mister Rogers' Neighborhood*, is a reality, which means both that individuals may personally encounter or experience it and also that neighbors have opportunities to show care for one another.

Difference in ability was also always close to Fred's heart. In another of the *Neighborhood*'s best-known scenes, Mister Rogers visits with a ten-year-old boy named Jeff Erlanger, who was living with quadriplegia and using a wheelchair. The scene takes place in front of Mister Rogers's television house—the house itself was not wheelchair-accessible—and they talk about Jeff's wheelchair and why he needs it. Together they sing "It's You I Like," a song sung frequently on the *Neighborhood*:

> It's you I like,
> It's not the things you wear,
> It's not the way you do your hair
> But it's you I like
> The way you are right now,
> The way down deep inside you
> Not the things that hide you,
> Not your toys
> They're just beside you.

But it's you I like
Every part of you.
Your skin, your eyes, your feelings
Whether old or new.
I hope that you'll remember
Even when you're feeling blue
That it's you I like,
It's you yourself
It's you.
It's you I like.[9]

On that day, Mister Rogers slightly modified the lyrics: instead of "not your toys," he sings, "not your fancy chair." During their conversation after the song ends, Mister Rogers refers to the lyrics when he says, "And I bet sometimes you do feel blue." Jeff acknowledges that he does, and they talk about what kinds of things help in those times. "I'm not feeling blue now, though," Mister Rogers says. "Me neither!" Jeff replies. The scene was filmed with little preparation and no rehearsal; Fred simply told Jeff that they would talk a little bit and then sing a song. The connection onscreen is natural, warm, and authentic, and this scene has moved audiences ever since. Fred greatly valued his conversations with people with disabilities—conversations he had frequently through the Make-a-Wish Foundation and similar programs, as well as personal connections.

———————

Fred Rogers's care about difference was rooted in his own history. Growing up, his parents worked at caring for those in their neighborhood and beyond who were in need—financial or otherwise. A revealing—and for Fred, very personal—example of this care was in the Rogers family's relationship with a young man named George Allen. Throughout Fred's childhood, his family employed African American domestic workers, and when Fred was four, the woman who worked for them died. Soon after, Jim and Nancy Rogers arranged for her teenage son, George, to live in their home, and he worked as their chauffeur and as a caretaker for Fred. George "spent lots of time with Fred throughout his childhood, introducing him to the wonders of jazz, photography, and airplanes," Long writes. George earned money playing drums in local dance bands, and he eventually used that money to take flight lessons at the Latrobe airport. He became a flight instructor, and when Fred was in high school, George taught him to fly a Piper Cub. (George later taught at the Tuskegee Institute in Alabama.)[10] This early experience of difference and need was incredibly formative for Fred. George wasn't, to young Fred, a "person in need"; he was a member of the household, an expert, a caretaker, and a teacher. But there was also an undeniable power difference. Though Fred's parents taught him, and later, his little sister, that all people should be treated with the same kindness and respect, George was still an employee of his family, without the bottomless resources Fred enjoyed as the white, eldest son of the wealthiest family in town. This example illustrates a tension always present in Fred Rogers's encounters with difference: he worked hard to build a *Neighborhood* representative of the difference he found essential and enriching in his own life, but as a person who was born with extraordinary power and privilege, he fell short, at times, of his own high standards. Fred Rogers *was* ahead of his time, but he wasn't *that* far ahead.

For example, François Clemmons recalls encouraging Fred to cast him and Betty Aberlin, a white member of the cast who appeared in almost five hundred *Neighborhood* episodes, as an interracial couple in one of the *Neighborhood* operas. Though Fred responded thoughtfully to the conversation, he never took that risk.[11] He also heard from viewers at times, as well as from François, that the choice to set the *Neighborhood* in the suburbs rather than in a diverse city was limiting. (*Sesame Street*, by contrast, represented a hip, urban center where people of many races interacted regularly, sometimes even as romantic couples.)[12] Still, the *Neighborhood* was by no means homogenous:

> Even in its first year of production, before Officer Clemmons appeared for the first time, *Mister Rogers' Neighborhood* had included segments depicting a black schoolteacher, a black master drummer, black pre-school and elementary school children, an interracial school, a black salesman, a black tap dancer, African folk dancers, a Chinese American scientist, a black florist, a Japanese origami artist, and Native Americans. It's not that *Mister Rogers' Neighborhood* did not have a diverse community even in its earliest days; it's just that viewers had to look for it harder than they did when they watched *Sesame Street*.[13]

Like his views on ethnic and racial diversity, Fred's views on gender had limitations that are sometimes apparent on the program itself. Early on, for instance, he wrote this song about moms and dads:

> I'd like to be just like my mom
> She's pretty and she's nice
> She knows just how to make the beds
> And cook things out of rice
> And Daddy likes the things she does
> The way she looks and, Gee!
> I'd like to be just like my mom
> And have someone like me

I'd like to be just like my dad
He's handsome and he's keen
He knows just how to drive the car
And buy the gasoline
And Mommy likes the things he does
The way he looks and, Gee!
I'd like to be just like my dad
And have someone like me[14]

To Fred's credit, he added spoken context when this song premiered in the third episode of the *Neighborhood*. After singing the song, as he's washing dishes, he says, "Well, you boys probably will be like your dads, and you'll do lots more things than just driving cars and buying gasoline. And you girls will probably be like your mothers too. Some mothers, you know, go out and work. They don't just make the beds and cook the meals. Lots of different things that happen in this world." In episodes 1083 and 1099 from 1970, the last two times Fred used the song on the program, he even revised the lyrics to eliminate most of the stereotypical language. Instead of Mom being "pretty" and "nice," she's "loving" and "bright," and instead of her knowing how to make the beds and cook, "she knows just how to care for me and works to make things right." And Dad, instead of being handsome, keen, driving cars, and buying gas, is "wise," "kind," and "knows just how to help me grow and does his work just fine." In that latter episode, B-roll footage plays during the song, showing both Mom and Dad active in providing for, playing with, and teaching their children. A shot of Mom pulling into the driveway (presumably coming home from work) as her kids wave hello to her from the window, and of Dad teaching his daughter woodworking (traditionally considered a male activity), are two subtle ways in which this segment undercuts gender stereotypes of the time.

But these decisions don't indicate complete enlighten-
ment. In 1983, Fred made a weeklong series of episodes on
daycare, and he marveled, even as late as 1999, at the need
for such a series: "If you had told me . . . twenty-five years
ago that I would've done a whole week . . . on childcare, I
would've thought, that's beyond my belief!"[15] Families with
two working parents were still a less-than-ideal arrangement,
in his view. And often, when he told the story of the beginnings of *The Children's Corner*, his ways of referring to its host,
Josie Carey, were less than fully respectful. In a 1989 interview, he answered a question about the show's format by
saying, "I wasn't on camera at all. This girl who was the secretary talked to all these puppets."[16] Though Josie was, indeed,
working as a secretary at WQED when the station started,
she was also an actress who had been performing for some
time, and she went on to host several shows, on educational
television as well as network programs, during and after the
Children's Corner years. Despite her impressive acting résumé,
somehow Fred continued to see her as a secretary.[17]

Fred also had his blind spots when it came to wealth.
Though he grew up in a charitable family and contributed to
causes he believed in throughout his life, he could be obtuse
about personal finances, especially those of the actors and
production team who worked for the *Neighborhood*. Long notes
that Rogers's holiday gift to Betty Aberlin (and likely to others
on his staff) was

> a card with a message indicating he had donated to a
> charity in her name. . . . Aberlin was struck by Rogers's
> apparent inattentiveness to the financial needs of his
> own staff, especially during the holiday season. She
> sensed within Rogers an indifference or ignorance to
> the material needs of his actors and crew—an attitude
> that became all too real when they looked at their mea-

ger salaries or felt the sting of no special bonuses at holiday time.[18]

Michael Horton, a close friend of the Rogers family over many years and an actor who worked on the program from 1983 to 2001, sees the source of this cluelessness in Fred's own perennial wealth: "When you come from a great deal of money and you never come from [need]—this is not the experience of 99 percent of people—you don't know what a person's struggle is to pay a bill or pay a mortgage, feed a family. . . . Life is a struggle for most people, and it always has been."[19]

Fred engaged and affirmed difference imperfectly, but his work was still extraordinary for its time, and it leaves no doubt about the value Fred placed on difference. For Fred, this value was rooted in his own history and theology. His experiences in childhood—and his parents' consistent care for the neighborhood—mattered greatly, but so did his most closely held beliefs about God and humans: all people are created by God, in the image of God, so all people are good. A diverse neighborhood, filled with a broad representation of the people God loves, was a natural and necessary response to God's inclusive love.

And this representation wasn't only a static, theological statement about God's world, though that in itself would have been worthwhile; it also had a social purpose in line with the *Neighborhood*'s core message, "I like you just the way you are." Fred intuitively understood that representation matters. It's more difficult to feel liked when you feel alone, and it's easier to feel alone when you don't encounter anyone like you. He never wanted children to feel excluded, so he worked at making sure they'd see others like themselves on his program: African American children could see Officer Clemmons, Mrs. Saunders, or the children in her class and see someone who shared their skin color; children with disabilities could see Jeff Erlanger or Chrissy Thompson, a girl who used leg braces and who visited *Mister Rogers' Neighborhood* several times in the '70s and '80s. Viewers could see themselves onscreen, so they knew that Mister Rogers was talking to them when he sang, "It's you I like."

It was also important to Fred that children experience people who are *not* like them. Long's book emphasizes Fred's belief that inclusion, love, and acceptance are roads to peace—not only on a personal level but also on a global scale. Children who experience difference and learn to respond to it with curiosity rather than fear will not grow into adults who make war when they are afraid. "Only by understanding our own uniqueness can we fully appreciate how special our neighbor really is," Fred said in a 1969 speech.

> Only by being aware of our own endowments can we begin to marvel at the variety which our Creator has provided in [people]. And as we do marvel we will find ourselves being concerned about the conditions that make life on earth possible, we will recognize the need to make people more important than things, and we will join hands with young and old alike by putting our dominant energies into developing a sane design for living.[20]

Finally, Fred embraced difference and shared it with his television neighbors because he saw those people whom society shuns as "the poor in spirit," a phrase used by Jesus in his Sermon on the Mount in the Gospel of Matthew (see Matthew 5:3, NRSV). Fred believed that those who are more obviously vulnerable—especially people with disabilities and children, but also those who are marginalized for other types of social difference—help others to connect with their own fragility. In the afterword to his friend Christopher de Vinck's book *The Power of the Powerless* (about de Vinck's severely disabled brother), Fred writes,

> Chris de Vinck's words reach into that part of me where tears are made and ever so gently help me to cry—and to wonder if there isn't a part of each of us which feels powerless and in need of unconditional acceptance. . . . Not all people are able to accept others— or themselves—in as loving ways as the people in this remarkable book. For those of us who are still trying, the message from the powerless seems clear: "Just be yourself and allow us to help you. . . . Our power comes in simply *being*. Yours can too."[21]

For Fred, people on the margins reveal deeper ways of being, where acceptance of self and others is built not on social capital but on simple existence. We are good because we are God's, and the "poor in spirit," those overlooked or outcast, help all of us to know this better.

In Tom Junod's definitive profile of Fred Rogers, originally published in 1998, he tells a story about Mister Rogers visiting a teenage boy with cerebral palsy. The boy had been abused early in his childhood, and now, as a teen, he struggled with self-hatred and self-harm. Junod tells the story this way:

> At first, the boy was made very nervous by the thought that Mister Rogers was visiting him. He was so nervous, in fact, that when Mister Rogers did visit, he got mad at himself and began hating himself and hitting himself, and his mother had to take him to another room

and talk to him. Mister Rogers didn't leave, though. He wanted something from the boy, and Mister Rogers never leaves when he wants something from somebody. He just waited patiently, and when the boy came back, Mister Rogers talked to him, and then he made his request. He said, "I would like you to do something for me. Would you do something for me?" On his computer, the boy answered yes, of course, he would do *anything* for Mister Rogers, so then Mister Rogers said, "I would like you to pray for me. Will you pray for me?"[22]

When Fred told Tom this story, Tom complimented him on asking the boy for his prayers, since this would surely make the boy feel proud and important. But Fred was confused by this response. "Oh, heavens no, Tom!" he said. "I didn't ask him for his prayers for *him*; I asked for me. I asked him because I think that anyone who has gone through challenges like that must be very close to God. I asked him because I wanted his *intercession*."[23]

People who are different, who have been marginalized by society, are spiritual teachers and friends of God; Fred Rogers wanted to be sure he lived side by side with them in his *Neighborhood*. And he wanted to welcome his viewers into the wide world of God's beloved, among whom they were most certainly counted.

HELLO,
NEIGHBOR

Finding Fred Rogers

14

PUPPETS AND PERSONALITY

I think I'll let the people see the comfortable inside of me.

L'essentiel est invisible pour les yeux. Fred often cited this favorite line from his favorite book, Antoine de Saint-Exupéry's *Le Petit Prince* (The Little Prince). Translated, it reads, "What is essential is invisible to the eye." For Fred, this quote expressed a truth about the neighbor—that we can't see, just by looking, what is most essential about another person[1]—and about God—that God is ever-present, whether or not we notice or name that presence.[2]

Fred himself was something of a mystery—at once very visible through his television work, but also private and enigmatic. Some of what was essential to him is certainly invisible; there are parts of his interior landscape we simply cannot see. Some of those invisible essentials may be out of view because he was complex and layered; some may be hidden because he chose to keep them that way.

Still, there's plenty that he *did* make "visible to the eye." There are clues to his personality and his interior life everywhere, and one cache of those clues is available on any visit to the Neighborhood of Make-Believe. The puppets that populate Make-Believe, Fred often acknowledged, are each aspects of his personality.[3] "Mister Rogers is Mister Rogers," said Don Brockett, who worked on the *Neighborhood* from its beginning until his death in 1995, but "Fred Rogers is Mister Rogers, Henrietta Pussycat, Daniel Tiger, Lady Elaine Fairchilde, X the Owl, and most certainly King Friday XIII. . . . I never fail to see these people in the real Fred that I know. . . ."[4]

Michael Horton, an actor on the *Neighborhood*, agreed with Brockett's assessment that King Friday is a key manifestation of Fred's personality. King Friday can be controlling and proprietary, and he sees himself as the authority on everything. Fred, too, had these personality traits, though he worked harder to finesse them than his fictional alter ego. Fred was known for being humble, and he made a practice of using "we" and "our" instead of "I" and "my" when talking about the *Neighborhood* and his work, but when it came to the specifics of the production, he was unusually—and even insistently—self-focused. For instance, during Fred's famous testimony defending public television funding before a Senate subcommittee, Senator John Pastore, who was chairing the committee, asked, "Do you narrate it?"

"I'm the host, yes," Fred replied. And in a kind of (admittedly slow-motion) cascade, he added, "And I do all the puppets, and I write all the music, and I write all the scripts—"[5] He didn't add that he controlled the whole thing obsessively, down to how many cuts he'd allow per minute of televised program.[6]

Fred knew he could be this way, and he had some work-arounds—ways to make his domineering streak more palatable to others without having to actually give it up. When he would make an assertion in conversation, he would sometimes follow it by saying, "Oh, Mister Rogers, get down off your soapbox."[7] Even watching himself onscreen, he might respond to a particularly insistent or earnest moment by raising one (substantial) eyebrow and saying, "Oh *really*, Mister Rogers?"[8] He knew his internal King Friday was very real, and that it gave him power and presence. "I hope that I'm not dictatorial," he said, referring to his work among the staff at the *Neighborhood* tapings, "but I also hope that there's a certain strength that is manifest."[9] And there was: his friend Tom Junod says that "In his own meek way, he was made of iron."[10] Still, Fred knew that that iron needed to be tempered, and perhaps this is why he wrote so many conversions into King Friday XIII's storylines. Friday might exert undue influence, wield unearned power, or overrule wiser counsel, but there is good news: he is capable of seeing a greater truth and, when he does, he can—without shame or defensiveness—turn and go in a new direction.

Lady Elaine Fairchilde is a Neighborhood of Make-Believe troublemaker of a different sort, and Horton sees her as a another very prominent part of Fred's personality. Fred called her "the mischief-maker, the fun-maker,"[11] and she gives expression to his ornery streak, which had been a part of him since he was young. He was known as a prankster in college, and even in his shy high school days, he sometimes sang "a rather raucous song during intermission at school dances about the beheading of Anne Boleyn."[12] Lady Elaine allowed him to play and push limits, even as he remained shy and reticent in his public life.

Lady Elaine causes an awful lot of trouble for the residents of Make-Believe—some of it even hurtful trouble. She upends the usual order of things, both figuratively, like when she transgresses typical gender roles or King Friday's established hierarchies, and literally, as when she uses her magical boomerang to turn the entire Neighborhood of Make-Believe upside down. Sometimes these literal inversions are expressions of Lady Elaine's anger or hurt, and other times, they have a helpful purpose—to get a kite unstuck from a tree, for instance. Lady Elaine's routine upending of the established order calls to mind a similar theme that characterizes the stories of Jesus in the Gospels and the teachings of many Hebrew Bible prophets: God takes the usual power structures and turns them upside down, filling the hungry, sending the rich away empty, casting down the mighty, and lifting up the lowly (Luke 1:46–55). It is these themes that are on view in the episodes where Fred himself took the greatest Lady Elaine–like, troublemaking risks—like the weeks on war featured in the previous part of this book. Admittedly, he stopped short of creating storylines that risked losing a substantial number of viewers, not because he worried for his paycheck or ratings but because he wanted to welcome as many children into the *Neighborhood* as possible.[13] At times, members of his team, including François Clemmons and Betty Aberlin, thought he should've gone further. Still, he took risks, sometimes quietly and sometimes quite boldly, and though he had no magical boomerang, he managed to turn things on their heads, much like his sometimes off-putting yet beloved puppet.

Fred's wife, Joanne, sees Daniel Striped Tiger as the puppet who most fully captures Fred's personality. Daniel represents Fred's shyness, fear, and self-doubt. In his earliest storylines on *The Children's Corner* and the *Neighborhood*, Daniel is a tiger who is tame but who sometimes worries about whether he has really mastered the urge to bite.[14] Later on, however, Daniel fears not that he is too aggressive but that he is too tame. In 1987, he and Lady Aberlin sang a beautiful duet on the program, "Sometimes I Wonder If I'm a Mistake." Daniel's part of the song has the following lyrics:

> Sometimes I wonder if I'm a mistake
> I'm not like anyone else I know

When I'm asleep or even awake
Sometimes I get to dreaming that I'm just a fake
I'm not like anyone else

Others I know are big and are wild
I'm very small and quite tame
Most of the time I'm weak and I'm mild
Do you suppose that's a shame

Often I wonder if I'm a mistake
I'm not supposed to be scared, am I
Sometimes I cry and sometimes I shake
Wondering isn't it true that the strong never break
I'm not like anyone else I know
I'm not like anyone else[15]

Fred wrote this song, which means that at some point he sat down and worked at finding the notes and lyrics, drawing these words from his own human experience. Daniel became a channel for the expression of Fred's own self-doubts and vulnerabilities: Was he a gentle person who still had to guard against his aggressive instinct? Or did he worry that he was too weak and mild, not strong enough to withstand pressure? Daniel reveals him to be both.

Other puppets also carry aspects of Fred's personality: Edgar Cooke sings everything instead of speaking; Henrietta is kind yet prone to fear; X the Owl is well-meaning but sometimes a bit clueless (Fred referred to X as his adolescent self); Corney is practical and entrepreneurial; Grandpère speaks French and offers wise counsel; Queen Sara is maternal and level-headed (and while she is modeled on Joanne, whose first name is Sara, she no doubt draws on Fred's personality as well). "The character of Mister Rogers has a fullness that only a child can completely appreciate," Sedgwick wrote. "During the Make-Believe portions, Rogers' character refracts into its component parts for all to see."[16]

It seems worth naming something else about this man who, to use Sedgwick's language, refracted into puppet personalities as a self-offering to the world: he was strange. Though many children did find him comfortable and comforting, he made some adults very *uncomfortable*. Some parents—often fathers—worried that he was too coddling or feminine. "I'm not John Wayne," he acknowledged in 1975, "so consequently for some people I'm not the model for the man in the house."[17]

For others, Fred's sincerity was unnerving. His insistence on being his honest self led to some surprising moments, like this one captured in Sedgwick's profile, from a break on set during a *Neighborhood* taping: "I stand nearby, watching. Our eyes meet. I approach him and tell him I like the raspberry color of his sweater. 'Oh, I love raspberries, don't you?' he says, smiling. I nod, my mouth suddenly watering. 'They're sort of . . . furry, though,' he adds, scrunching up his nose."[18] Another journalist noted a similarly odd moment, this one on screen: "A recent highlight of the program was taking an apple from his refrigerator and explaining to 5 million viewers that because he was on television, they could see the apple but not taste it. Then after making this observation, he just grinned a few seconds at the fruit."[19] Many viewers of Fred Rogers the person and Mister Rogers the host noted his childlike quality, which surely allowed him to connect with children while, at the same time, estranging him from some of his peers.

Michael Horton ascribes some of Fred's peculiarity to his unusual childhood. "A person who comes from a background like he does and was an only child for the first eleven years of his life, [with] incredibly doting parents and incredibly wealthy parents, [who] was driven to school in a limousine for his own protection because of the Lindbergh baby kidnapping—this is not something that most people can access. . . . This is how a person begins to be perceived as strange."[20] But importantly, in Horton's view, Fred's loving family and his unusual childhood also created much of what made him so appealing. And this observation is key: many of the very same things that made Fred Rogers so strange also made him magnetic; with so much to puzzle out, it could be hard to look away.

There's no doubt that Fred's deep spirituality also contributed to his otherworldliness. His daily disciplines and sense of God's omnipresence meant that he was tapped into the deeper mystery of the world, and he took that sense into every human exchange—whether in person or via television. Many people I spoke with about Fred commented on the intensity and focus of his presence—more on this in the next chapter. The writer Tim Madigan remembers the first conversation he ever had with Fred:

> In the first telephone call, at the end of an hour, a fairly long time for a celebrity to be talking to a reporter, he said to me—and it was a really amazing interview— but he said to me, "Tim, do you know what the most important thing in my life is right now?" And I said, "Well, Mister Rogers, we just met. How could I possibly know that?" And he said, "Speaking to Mr. Tim Madigan on the telephone."[21]

Madigan marveled, "He embodied the sacred presence from the moment he woke up in the morning until the time he went to sleep at night."[22] Once again, Fred's magnetic strangeness: most people do not experience the world this

way, and even those who operate with great spiritual awareness do not always know how to carry it into their day-to-day
interactions. It seems that Fred Rogers, by contrast, couldn't
help but carry it everywhere.

15

FRIENDS AND NEIGHBORS

There are many ways to say I love you.

Even the people who knew Fred Rogers best don't agree on who he was—not exactly. Tim Madigan believes he was a spiritual giant on the scale of Jesus or Gandhi, while Bill Isler emphasizes his normalcy and humanness: "I think what people get wrong about him is they want to make him unusual. . . . I think there are a lot of Fred Rogerses out there. Not with his talent, but with the care and concern. Where Fred would say, 'Look for the helpers,' I'd say, 'Look for the Freds.' . . . The talent he had was what was unique to me, not his attitude and care of people."[1]

Tim Madigan and Tom Junod were both journalists who interviewed Fred for a story and ended up with a lifelong friend, so I asked each of them a version of this question: Fred gave countless interviews over the years, and you in your career have interviewed countless people, so why did this particular interview turn into something more? In Tim's view, Fred made himself available to everyone, and only a few people took him up on his offer of friendship. Tom, on the other hand, remembers a telling exchange with Bill Isler, then the president and CEO of Family Communications, on a drive from Pittsburgh out to Latrobe, Fred's hometown. (Fred was riding in a different car so he could get some work done on the forty-five-minute trip.) Bill said to Tom, "So what do you think is going on here?" Tom replied casually, "I don't know. Fred's a friendly guy, a friendly subject." But Bill saw it differently. "Journalists come in and out of here all the time," he pointed out, "and . . . mostly they spend a day with Fred and that's the end of it. And Fred is extremely good at saying no," he added. "Fred has taken an interest in you. . . . There is something out of this friendship that Fred wants to see happen." In Tom's view, that "something" was a "a spiritual thing," a "matter of ministry." Tom believed that Fred "had, among his many, many talents, that talent of seeing human need. He saw that I needed something, and he was determined to provide it. And he did."[2]

Fred had a lot of friends, and though their accounts of Fred differ and sometimes even contradict, they all agree on one thing: Fred made them feel special. They might not put it exactly this way, but Fred gave many people the impression that they were singularly important in his life. Some of them explicitly say that they were probably Fred's closest confidant, while others imply it; there's a gentle jockeying for position among some in his inner circle. At the very least, this seems to confirm Fred's gift for paying attention. When he told Tim Madigan, during their first phone call, that there was nothing more important to him in that moment than that conversation, he was displaying this unique ability, the ability to perceive and honor what Tom Junod called the "sacredness of the human transaction."[3] Whatever moment he was in with another person—even if it was in a letter or an email—that moment was sacred and all-encompassing, and the other person sensed that and internalized it. Jim Okonak, Fred's cousin[4] and the director of the family foundation, told me that he was struck by a pattern at Fred's funeral: each of the many people who rose to speak about Fred said something like, "Fred was my best friend."[5]

Though these relationships were real and enriching in Fred's life, they also came with complication. Like anyone, he had conflicts with his friends and colleagues. Betty Aberlin, a collaborator and cocreator throughout the run of *Mister Rogers' Neighborhood*, disagreed with Fred at times. "Betty Aberlin is a brilliant person; the program would not have worked without her," Michael Horton said. "There were a couple of times when Betty felt she knew Fred enough to say, 'This might be offensive to handicapped people,' 'This might be offensive to women,' 'This might be offensive to gay people.'"[6] And Betty didn't hesitate to speak even more strongly when she felt she should, like in February 1991. She was concerned about the Gulf War and the *Neighborhood*'s relative silence on the matter, especially because Fred had decided not to rerun the episodes of Conflict Week (discussed in detail in chapter 12) because they had been controversial. In a fiery letter to Fred, Betty wrote:

> When I was young I remember hearing how the Jews were exterminated in part because good men and women did nothing to prevent it. Now the Iraqi people are being slaughtered and children in Israel and in the U.S.A. terrorized, traumatized, brainwashed, and placated. . . .
>
> Your decision not to refer to or air CONFLICT week, and to do all-purpose spots instead, when you might have influenced popular opinion to embrace the New Order of Christ's Kingdom of Peace—stunned me. It was what you did not do and did not say that offended

me. I strongly disagree with you. I continue to love and forgive you as I question my capacity to *collaborate* with you.

Your "restraint" will probably insure the longevity of the Neighborhood on PBS. Perhaps when the privilege of free speech has ended in the world Bush intends, dissent will still be permitted in Make-Believe.[7]

It does seem that dissent was permitted—in Make-Believe as well as in their real-world relationship—but maybe *only* permitted and never fully engaged. Fred wasn't particularly good at conflict. Though I'm sure his ability to handle disagreement grew over time from the *Children's Corner* days, he never got comfortable with it. As Joanne reported in 2018, he struggled with conflict even in his most intimate relationship. "We never got mad at each other that much—that we could express well," she said. "We just got quiet. Both of us handled it that way, and that's not the best way. It's good to yell sometimes."[8]

Fred's longtime friendship with François Clemmons seems to have taken a more satisfying path through conflict, though this may be due to François's graciousness more than Fred's facility. François joined the *Neighborhood* cast in 1968, and not long afterward, Fred gently confronted him about his sexuality. Someone—Fred wouldn't say who—had reported seeing François at a gay bar. "Now I want you to know, Franc," François remembers Fred saying, "that if you're gay, it doesn't matter to me at all. Whatever you say and do is fine with me, but if you're going to be on the show, as an important member of the Neighborhood, you can't be 'out' as gay. People must not know."[9] In further conversation, Fred emphasized that he didn't think less of François or believe him to be immoral, but the message was clear: François could not be openly gay and also be Officer Clemmons.[10]

"It was devastating," François remembered. "I felt so bad I wanted to die."[11]

Fred assured him that their friendship could continue no matter what François decided to do, but Fred urged him not to let his sexuality interfere with his work. "You need to decide just want you want in life," François remembered Fred saying. "Talent can give you so much in this life, but that 'sexuality thing' can take it all away. Faster than you could ever imagine. . . . You can have it all if you can keep that part of it out of the limelight."[12] Fred even went so far as to encourage François to get married.[13] François eventually did, but his marriage ended after a short time.[14] "That, to me, was the supreme disaster of my life," François said. But he clarified that Fred did not *require* that he marry in order to stay on the program. "He did not speak in those terms. I take responsibility myself for making that decision. . . . I weighed the odds and felt I could do it. Sometimes you gamble, and you fail. . . . It was a nightmare, not because I married a bad person, but because it was the wrong thing to do." François and his wife lived apart for several years. When she met someone new, she contacted him to ask for a divorce. He was delighted for her.[15]

Over time, François found a middle ground. He was not public about his sexuality or his relationships, but he was more open about them with close friends. His friends, Fred among them, knew that he was gay, and he occasionally brought boyfriends to the studio or to social events where Fred was present. I asked him if Fred ever acknowledged, later in his life, the earlier, more difficult time when he had encouraged François to remain closeted. Not directly, François said, but instead, Fred would invite him for dinner or to a special function and ask him if he'd like to bring a guest.[16] Though François hadn't ever felt *personally* rejected by Fred—indeed, he considered Fred a surrogate father, and still does—it was healing, over time, to feel that Fred received his sexuality in an increasingly open, affirming way.

———————

Like much else about Fred Rogers, his own sexuality seems to have been somewhat complex. Michael Horton says that people always ask him if Fred was gay,[17] and Michael Long was often asked the same question whenever he told people he was writing a book about Fred. (Each, for the record, responds with his own kind of agnosticism on the subject.)

There could be a number of reasons for this common question, Long writes. For one, he suspects that Fred's gentleness and "lack of machismo" might sometimes prompt the question.[18] Similarly, Fred's associate Eliot Daley thinks that Fred's gender presentation, which Daly describes as androgynous, led people to assume he might be gay.[19] Another possibility, Long suggests, is that these questions arise from the knowledge that Fred (and Joanne) had many gay friends, some very close. They also attended Sixth Presbyterian Church in Pittsburgh, which moved to become a More Light congregation during Fred's lifetime, a designation indicating their support of LGBTQ ordination and marriage before both were officially adopted by the Presbyterian Church (USA). Long also points out that Fred's counsel to François muddies the waters even further: in advising François of the dangers of being publicly gay, in recommending (straight) marriage and single-minded dedication to one's creative work, could he have been sharing his own strategy for success? It certainly wasn't uncommon at the time for gay men to remain single or marry women, Long recalls, keeping their same-sex attractions completely beneath board.[20] John Sedgwick offers yet another possible explanation: "[what] adults, in their blundering fashion, take for homosexuality is more likely something that could be called pre-sexuality, the sexual nature of children. Adults don't get that. But then they aren't meant to."[21]

Whatever their reasons, some of Fred's friends and colleagues do think he was gay. Others, including François, insist he wasn't.[22] Maxwell King's biography of Fred offers this intriguing quote: "In conversation with one of his friends, the openly gay Dr. William Hirsch, Fred Rogers himself concluded that if sexuality was measured on a scale of one to ten: 'Well, you know, I must be right smack in the middle. Because I have found women attractive, and I have found men attractive.'"[23] Though this statement should certainly weigh more than the impressions of friends and colleagues since it references Fred's own words, it is still a little difficult to parse. It could be read as Fred Rogers disclosing bisexuality, but it's important to note that he did not use that term, at least in this instance. And the quote's context is limited at best.

To my knowledge, no one disputes Fred's fidelity to his marriage. His correspondence makes clear that he and Joanne talked constantly, whether they were in the same place or one or both of them was traveling. There's no doubt that they companioned each other through life, and that there was great affection—and profound respect—between them. Speaking at a symposium on the family in 1975, Fred said that he wished television would show more "people emerging out of adolescence and becoming adults who can make a marriage— not that the marriage will be all smooth sailing—not by any means—but seeing the new growth which comes from the conflict and the striving. . . ."[24] Whatever the invisible essentials of Fred's sexuality, there are plenty of indications that his marriage was characterized by commitment and connection.

Still, Fred's sexuality, like much about him, is a little mysterious. Of course it doesn't do any good to assume things that we can't know for certain; Long is right to make clear that neither Fred's gentleness nor his friendships with gay people nor the dubious counsel he offered François Clemmons tell us anything conclusive. But it's also important to remember that Fred's sexuality, however he conceptualized it, was part of who he was—including his spiritual and theological self.

Christian tradition has a checkered history with sexuality, and Christians over time have certainly struggled—and still struggle—to enfold sexuality into what it means to be a person lovingly created in God's image. Too often, sexuality and the body itself have been treated as dangers worthy of fear and in need of restriction. The resources of the tradition, however, are much richer than the most frightened or restrictive parts of its history. The Christianity that Fred claimed teaches that God creates people in God's own image (Genesis 1:27), and the second chapter of Genesis depicts an enfleshed God who forms humans out of the soil and breathes life into their nostrils (2:7). Bodies, in other words, are both good and godly. While Hebrew and Christian Scripture includes rules and prohibitions related to sex, it also includes the book of Song of Solomon, a longform, sensual poem that unabashedly delights in sex and pleasure.

Of course, many Christians affirm the teaching that humans (and human bodies) are good creations in God's image, yet also believe sin has disrupted God's design for bodies and for sex. By contrast, Fred did not see same-sex sexual attraction or activity as sinful. He made that clear to François Clemmons from their first conversation about François's sexual orientation. Here, as elsewhere in his life, he was guided by the most affirming messages of his faith tradition. His friendships with gay people were openhearted and unconditional, and he offered quiet support to his congregation as it moved to become more welcoming of people of all sexual orientations.[25] Though he never marched or campaigned for these values, his openness was enough to attract the ire of Westboro Baptist Church, whose members and associates picketed

Fred's memorial service.[26] But even if Fred *had* believed same-sex sexual attraction or activity to be sinful, he likely would have offered the same support. Though Fred was a member of a denomination with robust doctrine about sin, he rarely spoke of it. He found focusing on goodness to be so much more efficacious than focusing on sin. After attending a worship service while traveling in 1975, he wrote an acquaintance about how difficult it was to find good news in the words of the preacher: "I'm weary of people who insist on trying to make other people feel bad about themselves," he wrote. "The more I look around me and within me the more I notice that those who feel best about themselves have the greatest capacity to feel good about others."[27] In 1998, while the country was obsessing over Bill Clinton's sexual relationship with Monica Lewinsky, Fred wrote about sin in another letter, this one to his friend Tom Junod: "Last week I woke up thinking how I would like to go on the air and say something like 'Whoever is without sin cast the first stone,' or 'The Lord's property is always to have mercy,' or some other outlandish thing, and then ask for a moment of silence to think about forgiveness for those who want it."[28]

More particularly, Fred's words and work make clear that he didn't fear bodies—his own or anyone else's. He carried his body with a freedom that looks childlike, but that freedom didn't come directly from his own childhood. Remember, Fred wasn't comfortable with his body as a child; it drew jeers and taunts, and at age sixteen, he disliked it enough to order a Charles Atlas bodybuilding kit in hopes of physical transformation.[29] Somehow, he must have cultivated the bodily comfort he showed as an adult. On television in front of millions of viewers, he often risked looking silly, like when he rode on a seesaw (episode 1658) or tried break dancing (1543). During filming for episode 1548, which first aired in 1985, African American folk singer Ella Jenkins taught Mister

Rogers a hand-rhythm game—"Head 'n shoulders, baby . . . one . . . two . . . three." Not far into the song, Mister Rogers "fumbled crazily," then got progressively more confused as the song continued. "Thoroughly confused and thoroughly missing the beat—but still trying very hard—he looked into the camera and, with the cast and crew back there holding their mouths and turning red and leaning on one another and trying their hardest to keep silent—like you used to do as a kid in church—he gave a great grin."

Following the take, Fred endured the crew's gentle ribbing as they all watched the video. At first, he watched stoically, and then, as his performance descended into chaos,

Fred finally broke up, laughing again.

It was okay though, he said. He didn't mind the scene, didn't think he should go and practice the ankles 'n toes part and then reshoot the scene; no, he really didn't mind being seen on national television looking so positively like a klutz.

"I think it's important that people know that some things can be difficult for some people to do," he said, and then he looked at himself in the monitor one last time, put his head in his hands, and shook his head back and forth. "I really didn't do it well at all," he said.[30]

Though Fred didn't talk overtly on air about sexuality— such talk would've been developmentally inappropriate, and also probably uncomfortable for him—he did broach the subject of sexual difference. He did so in a very Mister Rogers kind of way: with thoughtfulness and care, with affirmation, and in song:

Some are fancy on the outside.
Some are fancy on the inside.

Everybody's fancy.
Everybody's fine.
Your body's fancy and so is mine.[31]

The full song has three more verses that talk about being boys and girls, and each verse ends with that same key message: "Everybody's fancy. Everybody's fine. Your body's fancy and so is mine." In this song, Mister Rogers explicitly affirmed not only the bodies of his television neighbors, but also his own. He didn't fall into silence or shame about bodies or their sexual differences, as has long been a temptation to people who claim Christian faith. Instead, like the best messages of his tradition, he celebrated.

It's also important to note that Fred's message of self-acceptance, which he broadcast to every viewer of his program and every person he met, reached and moved people who were struggling with their own sexuality. Indeed, some of his words take on special significance when heard in this context—whether or not that was his intent. Consider the song "Sometimes I Wonder If I'm a Mistake," quoted at length in chapter 14. The song appeared on only one episode of the *Neighborhood* (1578), but the scene between Lady Aberlin and Daniel Tiger that includes the song is a powerful one.

"Lady Aberlin," Daniel begins. "I've been wondering about something myself . . . something about mistakes. I've been wondering if *I* was a mistake." Lady Aberlin is surprised and asks what he means. "Well, for one thing," he says, "I've never seen a tiger that looks like me. And I've never heard a tiger that talks like me. And I don't know any other tiger that lives in a clock." After a pause, he adds, "Or loves people.

"Sometimes I wonder if I'm too tame," he says. And then the song begins.

Hedda Sharapan, who has worked with *Mister Rogers' Neighborhood* and Fred Rogers Productions since 1966, loves to

145

point out that the structure of this song is significant. Daniel sings about his worries and insecurities, and then Lady Aberlin sings a reassuring response. But the song doesn't end there. The two parts join, and they overlap in a beautiful duet: uncertainty coexisting with reassurance.[32]

When the song ends, Lady Aberlin reiterates, "I think you are just fine—exactly the way you are."

"The way I look?" Daniel asks.
"Yes," Lady Aberlin replies.
"The way I talk?"
"Yes!"
"The way I love?" Daniel asks last of all.
"Especially that," Lady Aberlin assures him.

————————

"The truth is inside of us," Mister Rogers says toward the end of the hand-clapping Ella Jenkins episode, "and it's wonderful when we have the courage to tell it." Then he sings "The Truth Will Make Me Free" (see chapter 16) adding this benediction: "Are you discovering the truth about you? Well, I'm still discovering the truth about me. That's what we do as we keep on growing in life."

There's much we don't know about Fred's own sexual self-understanding. But whatever the contours of that invisible essential, he deserves what he offered to the world: acceptance just the way he was.[33] And he deserves the benefit of his own deepest beliefs: that God created us, that God called us good, that God came, in the person of Jesus, to show us it was true, that each of us is intrinsically holy. Or, as he so succinctly put it, everybody's fancy, everybody's fine.

16

FRED'S BIG FEELINGS

*The very same people who are mad sometimes
are the very same people who are glad sometimes.*

In 1972, Rev. Fred Rogers preached a sermon at his home church, Sixth Presbyterian Church in Pittsburgh. For the Scripture readings that day, he chose two stories from Jesus's life. In the first, Jesus is twelve years old, traveling with his parents to Jerusalem for the Passover festival, as he did every year. But this year, he stays behind in Jerusalem when his parents head for home. Since they are traveling in a large group of family and friends, his parents do not worry about his absence for a full day, assuming that he is nearby. Finally, they realize he must still be in the city they've left behind, so they return and search for three days before finding him in the temple, talking with the teachers. His mother chastens him: "Child, why have you treated us like this? Listen! Your father and I have been worried. We've been looking for you!" (Luke 2:41–48, CEB).

Jesus replies—and his adolescent tone is up for grabs here—"Why were you looking for me? Didn't you know that it was necessary for me to be in my Father's house?" (Luke 2:49, CEB).

Fred explained, in his sermon, that Jesus "grew through all the stages of becoming an adult human that each one of us grows through. He felt the pains of separations, the shames of being scolded, the joys of knowing that he was worthwhile, the frustrations of trying to convince people of the truth, as well as the angers that everyone knows."[1]

In the second story, Jesus is again at Passover in Jerusalem, though he is now an adult, probably about thirty years old. He enters the temple again, but this time he finds merchants selling animals to temple-goers to use for sacrifice, and he finds money changers exchanging pilgrims' foreign coins for temple currency—and probably skimming a little off the top. Neither of these practices was new; animal sacrifice was part of Hebrew worship rites at the time, and foreign currency exchange was necessary for standardization purposes. Still, Jesus is furious.

"He made a whip from ropes and chased them all out of the temple, including the cattle and the sheep. He scattered the coins and overturned the tables of those who exchanged currency. He said to the dove sellers, 'Get these things out of here! Don't make my Father's house a place of business'" (John 2:13–16, CEB).

"Jesus could *and did* have very strong feelings," Fred reflected on this story. "You see, I believe that Jesus gave us an eternal truth about the universality of feelings. Jesus was truthful about his feelings; Jesus wept. He got sad. Jesus got discouraged; he got scared; and he reveled in the things that pleased him.

"What if Jesus had just sat?" Fred considered. "What if he had let his anger or his Sonship with God go unannounced?

"We would've known no Christ."[2]

For Fred, Jesus's full humanness—which includes a full range of feeling—is key to God's self-revelation. In other words, if Jesus hadn't shown a full, honest range of emotions, then Jesus couldn't have shown his full humanness. And if Jesus hadn't shown full humanness, then Jesus's power to know and love people would have been limited too. Through the Incarnation—God taking on humanness in the person of Jesus—feelings are sanctified; because Jesus, who was God, had big feelings, those same feelings are now caught up in the divine life.

———————

Fred took the example of Jesus's life seriously when it came to feelings. He often quoted his mentor, famed child psychologist Margaret McFarland, saying, "Anything human is mentionable, and anything mentionable is manageable." So he worked to mention his feelings rather than deny them. He knew that, acknowledged or not, revealed or not, his feelings would find their ways to expression. And he wrote a song about that belief for the *Neighborhood*, one that draws on John 8:32, "Then you will know the truth, and the truth will set you free."

> What if I were very, very sad
> And all I did was smile?
> I wonder after a while
> What might become of my sadness?
>
> What if I were very, very angry,
> And all I did was sit
> And never think about it?
> What might become of my anger?
>
> Where would they go, and what would they do
> If I couldn't let them out?

Maybe I'd fall, maybe get sick
Or doubt

But what if I could know the truth
And say just how I feel?
I think I'd learn a lot that's real
About freedom.

I'm learning to sing a sad song when I'm sad.
I'm learning to say I'm angry when I'm very mad.
I'm learning to shout,
I'm getting it out,
I'm happy, learning
Exactly how I feel inside of me
I'm learning to know the truth
I'm learning to tell the truth
Discovering truth will make me free.[3]

Part of Fred's truth was that he experienced significant anger, grief, and self-doubt in his life—feelings not typically associated with Mister Rogers but that were very real for him nonetheless.

In Fred's speeches and books, programs and interviews, anger is everywhere. Take, for instance, his famous 1969 testimony defending public television to a Senate subcommittee chaired by the gruff Senator John Pastore. It's not about educational access or equalizing opportunity; it's about feelings—and more specifically, it's about anger. Fred talks about the need for children to explore appropriate expressions of their feelings rather than the haphazard, often violent problem-solving of the popular cartoons of the time. "I think that it's much more dramatic that two men could be working out their feelings of anger—much more dramatic than showing something of gunfire," Fred said.[4] And then he recited the words to a song from *Mister Rogers' Neighborhood*—one that eventually appeared on thirty-eight episodes:

What do you do with the mad that you feel
When you feel so mad you could bite?
When the whole wide world seems oh so wrong . . .
And nothing you do seems very right?

What do you do? Do you punch a bag?
Do you pound some clay or some dough?
Do you round up friends for a game of tag?
Or see how fast you go?

It's great to be able to stop
When you've planned a thing that's wrong,
And be able to do something else instead
And think this song:

I can stop when I want to
Can stop when I wish
I can stop, stop, stop any time.
And what a good feeling to feel like this
And know that the feeling is really mine.
Know that there's something deep inside
That helps us become what we can.
For a girl can be someday a woman,
And a boy can be someday a man.[5]

The charming book *Dear Mister Rogers, Does It Ever Rain in Your Neighborhood? Letters to Mister Rogers* includes an example of the way Fred often spoke with children about anger. In response to a boy named Alex who asked, "Mister Rogers, do you ever get angry?," Fred wrote,

> You wondered if I ever get angry. Of course I do; everybody gets angry sometimes. But, Alex, each person has his and her way of showing angry feelings. Usually, if I'm angry, I play loud and angry sounds on the piano. Or, sometimes I swim very fast, and that helps me with my mad feelings. I think that finding ways of showing our feelings—ways that don't hurt ourselves or anybody else—is one of the most important things we can learn to do.
>
> What helps you when you're angry? . . . I have always called talking about feelings "important talk."[6]

Fred's focus, most often, was on behavior: ways to express anger, and what to avoid—hurting self or others. But he also often explored anger's emotional intricacy, connecting anger to fear—not of the raging other (I find no evidence that he had a parent or grandparent whose anger frightened him in childhood) but of the self. "When we're very, very angry we're afraid we'll hurt even the people we love the most," he wrote.[7] And he suspected that children worry that if they do hurt those people, they might lose their love.[8] "The scariest thing in life is loss of love and it starts so early," Fred said in a 1984 interview, when asked about anger between parents and children. "I think that's one of the most frightening things in the world."[9]

Much more than the anger we experience from others, Fred concerned himself with the anger we find in ourselves. He found his own anger frightening—at least as a child, and arguably even as an adult. He didn't always handle anger very well, as in his (often-avoided) conflicts with Josie Carey, Betty Aberlin, or Joanne Rogers, but he wanted to be sure his viewers knew that anger was OK, even important. "[Anger] is a real feeling that comes again and again between loving people," he said, "and like every other feeling it can be used in the service of our growing."[10]

Though Fred's ability to express anger interpersonally seems to have been limited, he did find ways to express it in solitude, through music or swimming, as he told Alex and his other television neighbors. And anger also played a crucial role in Fred's life. When Fred first saw television, he was appalled—he was angry—at how it was being used. It was that anger that turned Fred away from seminary (for a time) and toward television. Fred took his anger and used it to fashion his vocation. In a much less public example, he took his anger about his son's experience in the Toronto hospital and used it to make health care in many places more child-centered and family-focused. Anger, for Fred, may have been uncomfortable, but he affirmed it and, in the long run, used it to become someone who could respond to great need in the world. When he spoke, as he often did, of using anger "in the service of our growing," he took his own message to heart.[11]

When I started to research Fred Rogers and talk with people who knew him well, I often asked them some version of this question: *It's easy to make Fred into an otherworldly saint, but what did you experience in him that showed you his humanness?* I expected to hear about foibles or failings, but instead, almost every person answered with a story of Fred showing deep emotion. Michael Horton told me about a time that Fred came to his house in tears. Fred explained to Michael that his and Joanne's housekeeper had cancer and was nearing death, and he asked Michael to go with him to the hospital to visit her.[12] Tim Madigan remembered the day that Fred called unexpectedly, and as Tim began to speak with him, he realized Fred was crying. Fred told Tim that his good friend, the priest and spiritual writer Henri Nouwen, had just died. "The sorrow was deep and palpable," Madigan said.[13] Amy Hollingsworth writes about Fred's grief following the death of *Neighborhood* music director Johnny Costa, who had been a part of the *Neighborhood* for nearly thirty years and Fred's friend even longer. When Johnny died, Hollingsworth writes, Fred felt "as if part of himself were missing; so much so . . . that Fred considered shutting down production of *Mister Rogers' Neighborhood* permanently. . . ."[14]

When Fred said in his sermon that Jesus wept, he was referring to a story in the Gospel of John. In it, Jesus learns that his friend Lazarus has died. He travels to Lazarus's home intending to raise him from the dead, but still, upon seeing the grief of his friend's sisters, "Jesus wept" (John 11:35, KJV). In Christian tradition, Jesus is associated with a passage in the Hebrew Bible book of Isaiah, which reads, "He is despised and rejected of men; a man of sorrows, and acquainted with grief . . ." (Isa. 53:3, KJV).

In his way, Fred too was a "man of sorrows." As a child, the shame, fear, and anger he felt about being bullied was accompanied by grief, and so he "cried through his fingers" at the piano. The adult Fred, Joanne Rogers recently said, was "a very sensitive person, and tears were available to him."[15] In his four-plus-page prayer at the funeral of his beloved professor, Dr. William Orr, Fred lingered on gratitude and on intercession for the needs of the wider world, giving just a brief mention of grief: "We bring our joys and challenges which only you may know, and we bring our griefs which only you can help us heal."[16] Grief wasn't a burden to be lifted or a problem to be prayed against. It lived among the intricacies of loss, waiting patiently for the work of healing, meanwhile, unperturbed. Fred loved the line in Samuel Hazo's poem "To All

My Mariners in One" that says, "We speak / cathedrals when we speak / and trust no promise but / the pure supremacy of tears."[17] Tears were gift and grace. Sorrow was acceptable for Jesus, so it was acceptable for Fred.

Fred's message of affirmation did not insulate him from his own experiences of self-doubt. At times throughout his adult life, he struggled with self-understanding and confidence in his work, even as the world offered him adulation. In a set of meandering handwritten notes, probably from his seminary days, Fred wrote, "'I wouldn't mind going if I knew who I was.' 'I wouldn't be afraid to meet people if I knew who those people were meeting.' How can we discover our identity? Why isn't it enough for [Christians] to say, 'I'm a child of God'?"[18]

Fred especially struggled in the initial work of creation, when he would write the scripts for the *Neighborhood*. When Fred would go into writing mode, Bill Isler told me, he would look terrible.[19] Fred talked about this struggle himself in an interview in 1982: "There are times when I get very low, especially when I go into my office and try to write," he said. "Sometimes I just agonize."[20] In a note to himself, written in 1979, his self-doubt is even more exposed:

> Am I kidding myself that I'm able to write a script again? Am I really just whistling Dixie? I wonder. Why don't I trust myself? Really that's what it's all about . . . that and not wanting to go through the agony of creation. AFTER ALL THESE YEARS, IT'S JUST AS BAD AS EVER. I wonder if every creative artist goes through the tortures of the damned trying to create? GET TO IT, FRED! But don't let anybody ever tell anybody else that it was easy. It wasn't.[21]

Fred's language gets religious here, and not just "tortures of the damned" (though that certainly conveys the suffering he felt); the language of agony connects to the story of Jesus, especially Jesus in the Garden of Gethsemane. On the night before he died, just before his arrest but after being betrayed by one of his closest followers, Jesus went to a garden to pray with his disciples. While his friends kept falling asleep in their grief and terror, Jesus prayed and "began to be grieved and distressed. Then He said to them, 'My soul is deeply grieved, to the point of death'" (Matt. 26:37b–38a, NASB). In Christian tradition, this story is commonly known as "The Agony in the Garden." Though I don't think Fred was trying—consciously or otherwise—to equate himself with Jesus, he was drawing on theological language and biblical story to express the anguish he felt. No matter how many letters he received from viewers whose lives he had changed, he was never fully convinced it was enough. Even if he knew he'd had some measure of success—the good, meaningful, making-a-difference kind—he never was sure if he could manage to do it again.

And he couldn't help but focus, at least sometimes, on the people his message hadn't convinced. In an address at Saint Vincent Archabbey in Fred's hometown of Latrobe, he told the story of the balloon man: "To the delight of people of all ages, Bruce Franco has fashioned animals and flowers and hats and trolleys out of balloons several different times on our program," he began. Then he told his listeners that he had received a call from Bruce's home just a month earlier. When he spoke to Bruce's wife, Alice, he learned that Bruce had been suffering for a while, that he had been hospitalized and then had come home only to attempt suicide. After a second hospitalization and a second homecoming, Bruce made another attempt and took his own life.

Alice told Fred that, during Bruce's hospitalizations and treatment, he kept saying, "Why would anyone want a balloon man?" Alice reflected, "Bruce could never imagine that he was so much more than he thought he was."

Soon after their conversation, Alice sent Fred a package containing something Bruce had made. Inside, "carefully wrapped in tissue paper, was a hand-crafted wooden cross—a crucifix really—with an understandably agonized expression on the one being [crucified]." Fred continued, "It's as if this man felt abandoned at the last ('Father, why have you forsaken me?') and had begun the final mourning toward Easter."

Here, Fred is connecting Bruce's experience of suffering with the agony and abandonment of Christ on the cross (see Matthew 27 and Mark 15), just as he has done more subtly in his own life. Fred ached when he learned that someone hadn't been able to hear his message of deep love and wide acceptance. But he was also able to extend the grace to Bruce that he struggled to offer himself: "All I could think as I looked at that gift was God, the source of all forgiveness and love, rising from the tomb waiting for all of us to recognize that love is stronger than anything, stronger even than death."

"I'm convinced that Bruce knows that now," Fred said. "Just as he knows now how God wept with him in his darkest hours and always valued him: the balloon man who made children smile, far beyond what Bruce was able to receive on earth."[22]

Fred Rogers is an icon of kindness, and for good reason. But to flatten him into a single trait, mood, or feeling would do a disservice not just to Fred and his emotional complexity, not just to his program and its emotional intelligence, but also to the faith tradition he claimed. He saw his own feelings—and the feelings of others—through the lens of the life of Jesus Christ, whose own emotional roominess made way for Fred's personal growth and his television ministry of wide welcome.

17

ALL GROUND AS HOLY GROUND

Keep us safe and faithful, God. Tell us what to do.

When Fred was a seminary student, he visited a church with some friends to hear a well-known preacher. After the service began, they learned that the well-known preacher was not giving the sermon that morning; instead, an eighty-plus-year-old supply pastor would be preaching. "Well," Fred recalled, "I've heard some octogenarians preach who were superb, but this man was not one of them. He went against every homiletic rule that we were studying in school. In fact, I think he delivered the most poorly crafted sermon I had ever heard [in] my life."

When the sermon "mercifully ended," as Fred put it, he leaned over to his friend to whisper his relief, but then he noticed she had tears in her eyes. "He said exactly what I needed to hear," she said to Fred. He was stunned. "That terrible sermon? Exactly what she needed to hear?" The experience taught Fred a lesson that he carried with him forever, one that transformed the way he saw his television work.

I thought about that for a long time, and finally I realized that I had come in judgment and my *friend* had come in need. The Holy Spirit was able to translate the words of that feeble sermon to speak to the need of my friend. . . . That experience changed my life. Ever since, I've been able to recognize that the space between someone who is offering the best he can and someone who is in need is Holy Ground. Even the space between the television set and the receiver in need (and who isn't in *some* kind of need) is Holy Ground.[1]

Fred McFeely Rogers was ordained by the United Presbyterian Church in the United States of America (UPCUSA) on a sunny, breezy day in June 1963.[2] His family and friends filed into the pews; eight ministers participated in the service; the mood was buoyant. The service brimmed with music—including an organ prelude by Fred's beloved Bach, a solo, an anthem, and hymns about God's faithfulness and love.[3] And there was a one-of-a-kind charge for the ordinand: to minister to children and families through the mass media.[4]

The Reverend Rogers never served a church, and because ordination in the UPCUSA (and its later merger) was tied to churches, this meant Fred had to appear before his presbytery from time to time to keep his ordination active. Fred's pastor John McCall remembers joining Fred for those meetings and speaking on his behalf multiple times.[5] In other words, Fred's ordination was important enough to him to be worth the extra effort it required.

Every day that Fred walked onto the *Neighborhood* set to film episodes of the program, he prayed the same prayer: "Let some word that is heard be yours."[6] He believed in the guidance of the Holy Spirit and that the Spirit "translates our best efforts into what needs to be communicated to [any given] person in his or her place of need. The longer I live, the more I *know* it's true," he said.[7] "I've seen it happen so often—what I present in faith somehow nourishes the viewer."[8]

Fred received countless letters that confirmed his belief. Men would write in to say that they had been skeptical, but then they watched with their children and they came to appreciate Fred's work, that he had made a difference in their lives.[9] Women would write to say what his program had meant to their children, like the mother who said her child used the same nonsense word for two things: his pacifier and Mister Rogers.[10] Teenagers would write to confess that they sometimes watched the program while they were babysitting and found it comforting.[11] Adults would contact the *Neighborhood* to say that they had experienced abuse in childhood, but that Mister Rogers had given them hope.[12]

The actress Lauren Tewes, who publicly struggled with cocaine addiction, found *Mister Rogers' Neighborhood* on a dark day and "[something] inexplicable happened inside of her, which Tewes later attributed to 'God speaking to me through the instrument of Mister Rogers.'"[13] Another woman wrote to say that Mister Rogers saved her life. Exhausted, depressed, and desperate, she was driving a car one day with her sixteen-month-old son in the back seat. As she sat at an intersection, she saw a truck approaching from the left and prepared to accelerate into its path. Then, from the back seat floated a voice—her toddler's—high and sweet. He was singing, "It's a beautiful day in the neighborhood . . ." She pushed the brake to the floor and turned off the car. She thought of life and love. She breathed, drove home, and got help.[14]

"How could a simple program like ours do all this?" Fred marveled. "But again, the Holy Spirit can use anything."[15]

In his essay "The Performance of the Pastoral," children's writer and illustrator Chris Buczinsky wrote, "Rogers is a pastor without a church, or better, one whose church has become the neighborhood."[16] Importantly, he didn't capitalize *neighborhood*. Fred's work on *Mister Rogers' Neighborhood* was only a slice of his ministry, and his viewers were only one part of his "congregation." Fred worked in formal ways to minister to his wider neighborhood, including in hospitals and in prisons. Along with a friend, he established a child-friendly visiting area in a men's prison, and his friend taught child development classes for the inmates. "The inmates who are the play monitors often say that their times with the children are the most humanizing times of their prison life," Fred shared in a 1994 speech. "When they can allow themselves to remember what it was like when someone loved and cared for them, they can care better for themselves even inside a prison."[17]

But Fred had yet another congregation among his friends and associates. And many of them noted not only Fred's general care and guidance but also a particular—and peculiar—form of his ministry in their lives. Fred had a way of showing up exactly at the right time, even if he had no logical way of knowing their need.

Nicky Tallo, who worked as floor manager on *Mister Rogers' Neighborhood* for many years, had this type of experience with Fred. "I'll be having some hard time, and the phone will ring," he said. "Afterwards, I'll hang up and say, 'I'll be goddamned. That was Fred Rogers.'"[18] Fred's friend, the writer Tom Junod, once said to Fred in an email, "No sooner do I send you an email this afternoon than I check my mailbox and find your messages. We've always had that, Fred, haven't we—what did hippies call it? Intersubjectivity? Or maybe just good luck."[19]

In reply later that evening, Fred wrote, "Yes, right from the start. And it's a blessing."[20]

Though he felt no need to belabor the point, Fred didn't think it was luck. For him, such seeming coincidences were the work of the Holy Spirit, so he tried to follow the nudges he felt. Fred believed God's action in the world was constant and purposeful, with a bias toward the marginalized and hurting; God acted—sometimes through him—to comfort the broken-hearted or accompany the outcast. In a 1985 interview, talking about the understated ministry of his show, Fred struggled to name his deep conviction that God works this way. "You don't need to speak overtly about religion in order to get a message across. . . . The people who are struggling are the ones who . . ."—and he let the sentence drop off. "I don't know why it's so difficult for me to talk about this," he continued.

> Let me tell you a story instead. Last week I had this very strong urge to visit a young woman I know who is pregnant and unmarried. I haven't seen her in a long time. Yet, here was this exceedingly strong urge to see her.
>
> We had a good visit, a long visit. Very near the end of our visit, she said, "Mr. Rogers, did you know this was my birthday?" I said, "No." She said, "I just wondered if that was the reason you stopped in."
>
> When I left, I was thinking God really cares about people who might seem like the outcasts of society. Why did I stop in? If it's mind reading, it needs to be called inspired mind reading.[21]

"Inspired," of course, is the key word here. Fred's belief that the "divine presence is everywhere"[22] extended even to human action. This doesn't mean that all human action is God-blessed or that Fred denied evil in the world. On the contrary, he felt and grieved evil, but he believed his life—anyone's life—could offer goodness: "With all the sadness and destruction, negativity and rage, expressed throughout the world, it's tough not to wonder where the loving presence is," he said. "Well, we don't have to look very far. Deep within each of us is a spark of the divine just waiting to be used to light up a dark place."[23]

So Fred traveled to Baltimore in 1987 when he heard about a young girl having brain surgery there and felt the nudge to go.[24] In 1968, after Dr. Martin Luther King's murder, he drove to the other side of town to François Clemmons's home, a couple of blocks away from where riots were happening. "I was upstairs in my apartment, but I was scared to death," François remembers. But then Fred appeared.[25]

Lisa Hamilton, who worked for *Mister Rogers' Neighborhood* as associate director of public relations and played Purple Panda in the Neighborhood of Make-Believe, remembers Fred's presence at a very painful time in her life. She and her husband, Scott, were both thirty-one years old when they learned that he had cancer. During the eight months of Scott's illness, Fred regularly came to visit, and he would pray with Scott, Lisa, and their son, Teddy. "I got the feeling he wasn't particularly comfortable praying aloud with people," Lisa remembers, "but he took it very seriously." Lisa was a religious person (she's now an Episcopal priest), and she believed that God had healed Scott. But one morning, she woke up, still holding Scott's hand, to find that he had died.

"I was really panicky," Lisa said. "And the doorbell rang."

When she opened the door, she found Fred standing there. Lisa remembers that he was licking his lips, which she said he sometimes did in situations where he felt uncomfortable.

"I was praying," Fred said by way of explanation, "and I felt you needed some help."

"So Fred Rogers is the person who called the funeral home," Lisa told me. "And he wept with me over Scott's body—the only person I remember weeping with me." Lisa also asked Fred about what to say to Teddy, and he offered gentle advice: make sure Teddy knows you will be there for him.

Fred read the Gospel lesson at Scott's funeral, and though Lisa didn't return to her job at the *Neighborhood*, Fred stayed in touch with her and Teddy for the rest of his life, sending cards or calling on Teddy's birthdays as X the Owl (Teddy's favorite puppet), on one occasion talking to Teddy's friends who were still at the house following a birthday party, and sending all of them autographed pictures at Teddy's request. Fred also spoke of Scott in a speech two years after Scott's death when he knew Lisa would be in attendance. He didn't name Scott outright, "but he mentioned courage in the valley of a shadow," Lisa remembered. "And I was so moved by that. I was just stunned. I was just stunned. . . .

"And that was such a kindness."

Years later, Lisa found out from David Newell—the director of public relations at the *Neighborhood* who also played Mister McFeely—that though Fred had shared the news of Scott's death with him and the other staff, he never told them about his timely appearance at Lisa's door. But this didn't surprise Lisa. "He did a lot quietly," she said. "So I feel that I am one of probably hundreds of people with stories like that."[26]

―――――――――

In 1994, nearly three years after Scott's death, Lisa Hamilton wrote an article for the *Christian Century* called "The Gospel According to Fred: A Visit with Mr. Rogers." Though it doesn't reference her personal life, the article does illumine some of Fred's theology that has everything to do with those appearances that fell somewhere between mysterious and miraculous. Fred told Lisa, "1 Corinthians 1:25 pretty much sums it up as far as my most influential theologian is concerned. . . . 'For God's foolishness is wiser than human wisdom, and God's weakness is stronger than human strength.' I can't imagine more surprising places for God to appear than a manger or a cross," Fred reflected. "Yet all through his life and resurrection, Jesus demonstrates the power of showing and sharing God's love."[27]

The "foolishness" language here is striking, and it echoes what Fred once said about hearing from some of those fathers who wrote to tell him his program had changed their lives: "It's kind of like what St. Paul says about being a fool for Christ. . . . God uses the strangest kind of vehicles."[28]

When Fred knocked on doors, made phone calls, booked flights, or got in his car in response to some nudging, he didn't feel heroic. He felt foolish. Maybe he was licking his lips every time. When he prayed or offered counsel, he felt awkward and inarticulate. But since he read his Bible every morning, he recognized the feeling. God in a manger or on a cross is foolishness. Listening and responding to the Holy Spirit is foolishness. Ringing someone's doorbell first thing in the morning is foolishness. And Fred was willing—even if not always comfortably—to be a fool: to speak through puppets, to fiercely defend childhood, to flout television convention, to welcome the outcast, to minister to the brokenhearted— sometimes in ways that beamed across America, and sometimes in the anonymous quiet of a living room.

"Each of us can be used," Fred believed, "in perfectly wonderful ways."[29]

18

HEAVEN IS A NEIGHBORHOOD

Goodnight, God, and thank you for this very lovely day.

The last week of *Mister Rogers' Neighborhood* episodes, which aired for the first time in August of 2001, was a celebration of the arts. Nowhere in the five-episode series does Mister Rogers acknowledge that it's the final week (though Mister McFeely and Mister Rogers did shake hands in the Friday episode—something they rarely did on the program—as an acknowledgement of so many years of creative and collegial friendship).[1] Instead, Mister Rogers closed Friday's episode in the usual way, knowing that earlier episodes would continue to recycle. For children watching, there was no emotional ending and no indication that anything had changed. Not so for Fred. Joanne said she thought he was a little depressed following the close of the show. When she asked him about it, he replied, "I miss my playmates."[2]

Only about a year and a half later, Fred and Joanne learned that Fred had stomach cancer. "When we got home after the tests and we knew what the story was, he just looked at me and said, 'Oh, I just hate putting you through this,'" Joanne remembered.[3] At first, Fred's medical team thought the cancer might be operable, but the doctors wouldn't know for certain until exploratory surgery began. Sadly, the surgeons found the cancer much more advanced than they'd hoped.[4]

Fred headed home. As a result of his extreme pain and exhaustion, he couldn't allow many visitors, which made him sad; he worried that people would think he was being elitist, "and he cried when he said that because he didn't want to hurt their feelings," his friend Bill Hirsch remembered.[5] Over the next few weeks, Fred struggled with pain, and his caretakers, including Joanne, struggled to find the right dosage of medication to balance pain management with his desire for lucidity.[6] Maxwell King's biography of Fred says that "when Joanne was helping Fred get back in bed, and trying to make him comfortable, sometimes he would smile sheepishly and ask for a hug."[7] During the final days of Fred's life, Yo-Yo Ma, a friend of Fred's for many years, called and played a Bach sarabande on his cello over the phone to comfort Fred.[8] Joanne said, "With us, with his family, he mostly talked about how grateful he was. He expressed appreciation for everything and told us how much he loved us. He said his goodbyes."[9]

On February 27, 2003, a month shy of seventy-five years old, Fred Rogers died. "When he went," Joanne said, "I could feel he went at peace and even with joy. I really feel he went with joy."[10]

Fred believed in heaven. When he spoke of his parents, grandparents, or other friends and family members who had died, he frequently said that they were "in heaven now." He believed heaven was a place of the kind of acceptance and wide inclusion that he saw at the heart of the Christian faith. "I believe we participate in eternal life through the grace of

God," he wrote in a 1978 letter. "We are accepted as we are and loved exactly as we are. In other words, I believe that heaven is sheer gift."[11] Over the course of his life, Fred learned a great deal about other religions and became increasingly open to their wisdom. His faith was a generous one, though always rooted in Christianity. Near the end of his life, in 2000, he professed a view of heaven built on that same love and welcome that he had claimed in 1978: "When I think about heaven, it is a state in which we are so greatly loved that there is no fear and doubt and disillusionment and anxiety. It is where people really do look at you with those eyes of Jesus."[12]

I don't know that Fred ever identified himself as a universalist—someone who believes everyone is included in God's salvation—but the beliefs he did share about heaven seem to point this way. He was good friends with Johnny Costa, the musical director of *Mister Rogers' Neighborhood* and an acclaimed jazz pianist. Johnny was a kidder, often irreverent or profane, and writer John Sedgwick described him as a "chipper" man who "might be a Marx Brother."

> It would be a very different Neighborhood without Johnny Costa. His repertory runs freely from ragtime to Rachmaninoff, all of it played with quick hands and a light touch. Unusually for television, the Neighborhood shows are all taped live to Costa's music, making him the program's true director, to the actual director's occasional frustration. Costa supplies much of the show's timing, and with his improvisations, he catches the mood of each segment. I once suggested to Rogers that Costa's music is the Holy Spirit. "That's a very sensitive observation," he replied.[13]

Johnny didn't disagree. "'Show me a picture or give me some words, and it just comes,' he [said], shrugging his shoulders. 'I don't know why. I think it comes from upstairs. I really do. I don't mean that I have a direct line . . . but . . . I mean, it just happens. Sometimes it amazes *me*. Because I'm not like . . . I'm not a holy person . . . you know?'"[14]

Johnny worried, sometimes, about his own eternal destination, and he'd talk to Fred about his concerns.

> Johnny says that he and Fred Rogers often talk about where you go when you die, Johnny being particularly concerned with just how forgiving the gates of heaven are. "I tell Fred that I'm afraid sometimes," he explains, calmly, not uncomfortable with the topic. "Afraid about some of my sins, you know, throughout my life. I tell him that I think I'm more bad than good sometimes. I say that I'm thinking about hell," he explains.
>
> Fred Rogers tells Johnny Costa not to worry too much about going to hell. "Remember your music," he will say to him. "Remember how you give this great comfort to people through your music."[15]

When Fred spoke of his friend Bruce Franco, the balloon man who died by suicide, it was clear he believed that Bruce was ushered into the welcome of God.[16] Where some Christians with more narrow views of heaven would challenge the forgivability of suicide, Fred believed that nothing was beyond God's mercy. In fact, in 2001, walking down the street in Pittsburgh after his daily swim, Fred was stopped by a man he didn't know who was in the midst of a debate with his co-workers about salvation. "Tell these people there's only one way to God," the man demanded. But Fred replied simply, "God loves you just the way you are."[17]

Fred was serious about heaven's wide welcome, but he could also be whimsical about the afterlife. When a friend of his from high school named Ned Nakles died, he mentioned

in a 5 a.m. email to Tom Junod that he and Joanne were traveling to Latrobe for the funeral. "There's the most beautiful full
moon this morning," he added at the end of the note. "I think
Ned hung it there sometime during the night."[18] Fred also
found heaven, not surprisingly, in music. In a 1999 interview,
he said, "I drive along, you know, in my car, and sometimes
I'll put on one of [Yo-Yo Ma's] tapes that is an unaccompanied
suite of Bach and I think, this must be what heaven is like."[19]
Perhaps Fred accessed this same transcendence when Yo-Yo
Ma played for him over the phone as Fred neared death.

Shortly before Fred lost consciousness in February 2003, he
asked Joanne, "Do you think I'm a sheep?"[20] As he did in so
many parts of his life, Fred was connecting his lived experience
to the biblical story. This time, however, the connection was
darker. In Matthew 25:31–46 (CEB), in an apocalyptic teaching
sometimes referred to in Christian tradition as the "Judgment
of the Nations," Jesus says that "when the Human One [or Son
of Man, a reference to Jesus] comes in his majesty and all his
angels are with him, he will sit on his majestic throne." He will
judge the nations, the teaching goes, separating them "just as
a shepherd separates the sheep from the goats." The king will
put the sheep on his right; the goats he will put on his left.

Then the sheep will be welcomed and praised: "Inherit
the kingdom that was prepared for you before the world began." And the king will explain their inheritance this way:
"I was hungry and you gave me food to eat. I was thirsty and
you gave me a drink. I was a stranger and you welcomed
me. I was naked and you gave me clothes to wear. I was sick
and you took care of me. I was in prison and you visited me."

This welcome, Jesus says, will confuse the sheep. They
will ask, "Lord, when did we see you hungry and feed you,

or thirsty and give you a drink? When did we see you as a stranger and welcome you, or naked and give you clothes to wear? When did we see you sick or in prison and visit you?" And the Son of Man will reply, "I assure you that when you have done it for one of the least of these brothers and sisters of mine, you have done it for me."

The goats—well, it won't go so well for them. According to Jesus, the king's words will be downright harsh: "Get away from me, you who will receive terrible things. Go into the unending fire that has been prepared for the devil and his angels. I was hungry and you didn't give me food to eat. I was thirsty and you didn't give me anything to drink. I was a stranger and you didn't welcome me. I was naked and you didn't give me clothes to wear. I was sick and in prison, and you didn't visit me."

Of course, Jesus says, the goats will object. "Lord, when did we see you hungry or thirsty or a stranger or naked or sick or in prison and didn't do anything to help you?" And the king will reply in just the same way he replied to the sheep—with one crucial difference: "I assure you that when you *haven't* done it for one of the least of these, you *haven't* done it for me" (emphasis added).

"And they will go away into eternal punishment," Jesus says. "But the righteous ones will go into eternal life."

When Fred asked Joanne if he was a sheep, he was asking whether she thought he would be welcomed into the inheritance, whether he had measured up, whether his love was tangible enough to have served the king about whom Jesus spoke. Fred Rogers wasn't the first—or the last—person to be a little terrified by this passage. It's not a very universalist portrayal of God's response to human fallibility—though there are other parts of the Bible that suggest more merciful ultimate realities. Still, this is a man who spent his whole life affirming the goodness of others, who assured the uncertain Johnny Costa and defended God's generous love to strangers on the street. Yet, nearing death, when it came to his own fragile self, he wasn't 100 percent sure. At the end of his life, at least for a moment, Fred questioned his own deepest gospel.

No one else did, though. In reply to Fred's question, Joanne said, "Fred, if ever there was a sheep, you're one."[21] And when news of his death was shared with the public, people everywhere sent messages of gratitude and farewell. An anonymous writer said, "If it's possible, heaven became an even better neighborhood today."[22] Pittsburgh Theological Seminary, of which Fred was an alumnus, said, "We rejoice in our sure hope that he lives again, in the very neighborhood of God."[23]

———————————

Ultimately, that's exactly what Fred believed: that heaven is a neighborhood. The neighborhoods he worked to build on earth were modeled not only on the neighborhoods of his own growing but also on the neighborhood of heaven. In heaven, he believed, we are met with the love and grace that we can only fallibly extend in this life. There, he professed, we are surrounded by the neighbors who came before us—the "communion of saints," in Christian language.

At the end of many of his speeches, Fred would invite his listeners to spend a minute with him in silence. He'd say something like this:

> My hunch is that everyone who has ever graduated from a college or a university or a seminary, anyone who has ever been able to sustain a good work, has had at least one person—and often many—who have believed in him or her. We just don't get to be competent human beings without a lot of different investments from others . . . often quite invisible to the eye. I'd like to give you an

invisible gift: a gift of a silent minute to think about
anyone who has helped you to become who *you* are today—any people you know who have been an important part of your journey. Some of them may be here
right now. Some might be far away. Some may even be
in heaven. But wherever they are—if they've loved you
and encouraged you, and wanted what was best in life
for you, they're right inside yourself, and I just feel that
you deserve time on this very special occasion to devote
some thought to them. So let's take a minute—a minute
of silence—and think about the people who have loved
us all along the way, the people who have helped us
become who we are. One minute. I'll watch the clock.[24]

I've thought a lot about why Fred did this. I think it had
something to do with humility, with realizing that none of us ac-
complishes anything solely by our own merits. It also had something to do with gratitude, and I suspect he hoped people would
leave his speech and thank whomever they'd remembered. Fred
also relished silence, so he took joy in offering a gift of silence
to a loud world. But this was also a way of calling to mind the
communion of saints, the whole, wide collection of God's people, dead and alive, who surround each of us. The neighborhood
of Fred's imagination, in other words, was a neighborhood that
stretched not only to people of many races, genders, ability lev-
els, socioeconomic groups, and sexualities; not only to tangible
neighbors as well as to television neighbors; not only to the joyful and the despondent; but also, ultimately, to both the living
and the dead. The neighborhood of Fred's imagination was God's
neighborhood, where heaven and earth, the human and the divine, are brought together in the generous love of Christ.

"Frankly," Fred once said, "I think that after we die, we
have this wide understanding of what's real. And we'll probably say, 'Ah, so that's what it was all about.'"[25]

NOTES

The unnumbered citation at the beginning of each chapter's notes refers to the epigraph. FRA stands for the Fred Rogers Archive, housed at the Fred Rogers Center for Early Learning and Children's Media at Saint Vincent College in Latrobe, Pennsylvania.

Introduction

"Why Hi Song," words by Josie Carey and music by Fred M. Rogers, 1954, © The McFeeley-Rogers Foundation.

1. Tom Junod, interview by the author, February 6, 2018.

2. Fred Rogers cites these words of Joanne Rogers in an interview by Karen Herman, Television Academy Foundation, July 22, 1999, https://interviews.televisionacademy.com/interviews/fred-rogers.

3. James Kaplan, "The Good Neighbor," *TV Guide*, October 26–November 1, 1996, quoted in Amy Hollingsworth, *The Simple Faith of Mister Rogers* (Nashville: Thomas Nelson, 2007), xxviii.

4. James R. Okonak, interview by the author, September 12, 2017.

5. John Rogers, in an interview from *Won't You Be My Neighbor?*, directed by Morgan Neville (Los Angeles: Universal Studios Home Entertainment, 2018), DVD.

6. Betsy Weaver, "Mr. Rogers: There's No Movie Star Here," *Boston Parents Paper*, July 1986, 8, the Fred Rogers Archive (FRA) at the Fred Rogers Center, St. Vincent College, Latrobe, Pennsylvania.

7. John E. Fitzgerald, "Mr. Rogers: Gentle Apostle," *Our Sunday Visitor: National Catholic Family Weekly*, August 29, 1971, 2, Mr. Rogers' Neighborhood Collection, 1955–2003, SC.1989.07, Archives & Special Collections, University of Pittsburgh Library System.

8. Lisa Belcher-Hamilton, "The Gospel according to Fred: A Visit with Mr. Rogers," *Christian Century*, April 13, 1994.

9. James Breig, "Mister . . . Er, Reverend . . . Rogers Chats about His Young Neighbors," *The Evangelist: Official Publication of the Diocese of Albany*, June 20, 1974, 5-B, FRA.

10. Tim Madigan, interview by the author, March 19, 2018.

11. Belcher-Hamilton, "The Gospel according to Fred."

1. Childhood, Love, and Fear

"Are You Brave?" words and music by Fred M. Rogers, 1986, © The McFeeley-Rogers Foundation.

1. John Sedgwick, "Who the Devil Is Fred Rogers?," *Wigwag*, November 1989, 31–32, FRA.

2. The narrative that follows in this section is drawn from Fred Rogers, "More Than We Know" (address, Opening Ceremonies of the Sesquicentennial of Saint Vincent, Saint Vincent Archabbey Basilica, Latrobe, PA, April 25, 1995), FRA.

3. This would have been the most direct route to take from the Second Ward School to the Rogers family's home on Weldon Street, though I don't know for certain that he took this route.

4. One of Fred's classmates remembered years later that the only sign of the Rogers's family's extraordinary wealth was that Fred owned seven pairs of corduroy pants. See John Sedgwick, "Who the Devil Is Fred Rogers?," 31. I don't know whether he was wearing a pair the day he was chased, but he may have been.

5. Rogers, "More Than We Know."

6. Rogers, "More Than We Know."

7. Fred Rogers, speech to the American Academy of Pediatrics, New York City, July 19, 1989, FRA.

8. Amy Hollingsworth, *The Simple Faith of Mister Rogers: Spiritual Insights from the World's Most Beloved Neighbor* (Nashville: Thomas Nelson, 2007), 136.

9. Rogers, "More Than We Know."

10. Rogers, speech to the American Academy of Pediatrics.

11. Sedgwick, "Who the Devil Is Fred Rogers?," 30–31.

12. John E. Fitzgerald, "Mr. Rogers: Gentle Apostle," *Our Sunday Visitor: National Catholic Family Weekly*, August 29, 1971, 2–3, Mr. Rogers' Neighborhood Collection, 1955–2003, SC.1989.07, Archives & Special Collections, University of Pittsburgh Library System.

13. Fred Rogers, "The Boundaries of Freedom" (Sermon, Sixth Presbyterian Church, Pittsburgh, August 27, 1972), 5, FRA.

2. The First Neighborhood

"Won't You Be My Neighbor?," words and music by Fred M. Rogers, 1967, © The McFeeley-Rogers Foundation.

1. James R. Okonak, interview by the author, September 12, 2017.

2. John Sedgwick, "Who the Devil Is Fred Rogers?," *Wigwag*, November 1989, 31, FRA.

3. Okonak, interview by the author.

4. Fred Rogers, interview by Karen Herman, Television Academy Foundation, July 22, 1999, https://interviews.televisionacademy.com/interviews/fred-rogers.

5. Fred Rogers, speech for migrant workers, April 27, 1987, FRA, quoted in Michael G. Long, *Peaceful Neighbor: Discovering the Countercultural Mister Rogers* (Louisville: Westminster John Knox, 2015), 100.

6. Okonak, interview by the author.

7. Maxwell King, *The Good Neighbor: The Life and Work of Fred Rogers* (New York: Harry N. Abrams, 2018), 38.

8. Rogers, Television Academy Foundation interview.

9. Okonak, interview by the author.

10. "The Biography of Fred Rogers," Fred Rogers Productions, March 12, 2014, https://vimeo.com/88897046.

11. "History," Latrobe Area Historical Society (website), accessed November 13, 2018, http://www.greaterlatrobe.net/history/history.htm.

12. Okonak, interview by the author.

3. Adolescence and Acceptance

"I Like You as You Are," words by Josie Carey and music by Fred M. Rogers, 1959, © The McFeeley-Rogers Foundation.

1. John Sedgwick, "Who the Devil Is Fred Rogers?," *Wigwag*, November 1989, 31, FRA.

2. Fred Rogers, "Latrobe High School Baccalaureate Speech" (Latrobe, PA, June 2, 1996), FRA.

3. Fred Rogers, interview by Karen Herman, Television Academy Foundation, July 22, 1999, https://interviews.televisionacademy.com/interviews/fred-rogers.

4. Fred Rogers, "Latrobe High School Baccalaureate Speech."

5. Sedgwick, "Who the Devil Is Fred Rogers?," 31. This was over a decade before the McFeely-Rogers Foundation financed the construction of a public in-ground pool for Latrobe.

6. Sedgwick, "Who the Devil Is Fred Rogers?," 32.

7. Tim Madigan, *I'm Proud of You: My Friendship with Fred Rogers* (self-pub., CreateSpace, 2012), 19.

8. Maxwell King, *The Good Neighbor: The Life and Work of Fred Rogers* (New York: Harry N. Abrams, 2018), 46.

9. Rogers, Television Academy Foundation interview.

10. "I Like You as You Are," 1959, words by Josie Carey and music by Fred M. Rogers, © The McFeeley-Rogers Foundation, http://www.neighborhoodarchive.com/music/songs/i_like_you_as_you_are.html.

11. Fred Rogers, "*Protestant Hour* Broadcast Script" (radio, February 25, 1976), 2–3, FRA.

12. Fred Rogers, commencement speech at Middlebury College, May 2001, Series VII, Final Projects 2001–2003, Subseries G, Speeches, FRA, quoted in Michael G. Long, *Peaceful Neighbor: Discovering the Countercultural Mister Rogers* (Louisville: Westminster John Knox, 2015), 30.

13. Fred Rogers, speech at Grove City, PA, June 13, 1979, CW10, folder "Lynch, Elaine: Daily file—June 1979," FRA, quoted in Long, *Peaceful Neighbor*, 31.

14. Tom Junod, "Can You Say . . . Hero?," *Esquire*, November 1998 (republished April 6, 2017), https://www.esquire.com/features /can-you-say-hero-esq1198.

15. Joanne Rogers, in an interview from *Won't You Be My Neighbor?*, directed by Morgan Neville (Los Angeles: Universal Studios Home Entertainment, 2018), DVD.

16. Patricia Abrames, letter to Fred Rogers, undated, Mr. Rogers' Neighborhood Collection, 1955–2003, SC.1989.07, Archives & Special Collections, University of Pittsburgh Library System.

17. Linda Ann Meise, letter to Fred Rogers, June 6, 1972, Mr. Rogers' Neighborhood Collection, 1955–2003, SC.1989.07, Archives & Special Collections, University of Pittsburgh Library System.

18. Anna K. Church, letter to Fred Rogers, March 29, 1973, Mr. Rogers' Neighborhood Collection, 1955–2003, SC.1989.07, Archives & Special Collections, University of Pittsburgh Library System.

4. College Years, Loneliness, and Musical Expression

"The Truth Will Make Me Free," words and music by Fred M. Rogers, 1970, © The McFeeley-Rogers Foundation.

1. Maxwell King, *The Good Neighbor: The Life and Work of Fred Rogers* (New York: Harry N. Abrams, 2018), 48–50.

2. Fred Rogers, interview by Karen Herman, Television Academy Foundation, July 22, 1999, https://interviews.televisionacademy.com /interviews/fred-rogers.

3. Melanie Chadwick Stevens, "Mr. Rogers' Neighborhood," *Parents Magazine*, May 1982, 78, FRA.

4. Rogers, Television Academy Foundation interview.

5. Joanne Rogers, Fred Rogers Center Oral History Project interview by Jessica Wierderhorn, Narrative Trust, June 14, 2007, 12–13, quoted in Margaret Mary Kimmel and Mark Collins, "The Wonder of It All: Fred Rogers and the Story of an Icon" (Fred Rogers Center, September 2008), FRA.

6. Joanne Rogers, Oral History Project interview.

7. Rogers, Television Academy Foundation interview.

8. Audrey St. Clair, "Rollins Walking Tour Celebrates Mister Rogers," Rollins360, February 20, 2018, https://360.rollins.edu/arts -and-culture/rollins-walking-tour-celebrates-mister-rogers.

9. "The State You're In: Mr. Rogers Found Calling of 'Service' in

Winter Park," March 27, 2018, http://www.tampabay.com/news/The
-State-You-re-In-Mr-Rogers-found-calling-of-service-in-Winter-Park_16
6675671.

10. Michael Long points out that this group was taking an ac-
commodationist approach, "addressing race-specific problems not by
calling for desegregation but rather by seeking to improve the quality
of racially segregated institutions." Still, Long notes, the context is
important: "Rollins was such a bastion of Southern white privilege
that the work undertaken by Rogers and his committee must have appeared to some of his fellow students as downright radical." Michael G.
Long, *Peaceful Neighbor: Discovering the Countercultural Mister Rogers* (Louisville: Westminster John Knox, 2015), 82–83.

11. King, *The Good Neighbor*, 60.

12. "The State You're In."

13. Rogers, Television Academy Foundation interview.

14. Avery Chenoweth, "Let's Hear It for Latrobe, Pa.," *Mid–Atlantic
Country*, April 1986, 54, Mr. Rogers' Neighborhood Collection, 1955–
2003, SC.1989.07, Archives & Special Collections, University of Pittsburgh Library System.

15. John Sedgwick, "Who the Devil Is Fred Rogers?," *Wigwag*, November 1989, 32, FRA.

16. King, *The Good Neighbor*, 41–42.

17. Stevens, "Mr. Rogers' Neighborhood," 77.

18. Stevens, "Mr. Rogers' Neighborhood," 77–78.

19. Amy Kaufman, "Fred Rogers' Family Keeps the Legacy of 'Mister Rogers' Neighborhood' Alive with a Candid New Documentary,"
Los Angeles Times, June 12, 2018, http://www.latimes.com/entertainment
/movies/la-et-mn-mister-rogers-family-neighborhood-documentary
-20180612-story.html.

20. *Mister Rogers' Neighborhood*, episode 1550, originally broadcast
May 17, 1985.

21. Sedgwick, "Who the Devil Is Fred Rogers?," 32.

22. Rogers, Television Academy Foundation interview.

5. Formation in New York City

"You're Growing," words and music by Fred M. Rogers, 1967, ©
The McFeeley-Rogers Foundation.

1. Fred Rogers, in an interview by Amy Hollingsworth, from Amy Hollingsworth, *The Simple Faith of Mister Rogers: Spiritual Insights from the World's Most Beloved Neighbor* (Nashville: Thomas Nelson, 2007), xxii.

2. Fred Rogers, interview by Karen Herman, Television Academy Foundation, July 22, 1999, https://interviews.televisionacademy.com/interviews/fred-rogers.

3. Maxwell King, *The Good Neighbor: The Life and Work of Fred Rogers* (New York: Harry N. Abrams, 2018), 73.

4. Joanne Rogers, in the foreword to Fred Rogers, *The World According to Mister Rogers: Important Things to Remember* (New York: Hachette Books, 2003), 3.

5. King, *The Good Neighbor*, 75.

6. Amy Kaufman, "Fred Rogers' Family Keeps the Legacy of 'Mister Rogers' Neighborhood' Alive with a Candid New Documentary," *Los Angeles Times*, June 12, 2018, http://www.latimes.com/entertainment/movies/la-et-mn-mister-rogers-family-neighborhood-documentary-20180612-story.html.

7. Rogers, Television Academy Foundation interview.

8. Fred Rogers, "Here," email message to Tom Junod, August 23, 1998, FRA.

9. Fred Rogers, "Re: Reaction," email message to Tom Junod, October 26, 1998, FRA.

10. Fred Rogers, "Re: A True American Hero," email message to Tom Junod, November 16, 1998, FRA.

11. Tim Madigan, *I'm Proud of You: My Friendship with Fred Rogers* (self-pub., CreateSpace, 2012), 66.

12. Rogers, Television Academy Foundation interview.

13. Rogers, Television Academy Foundation interview.

14. John McCall, interview by the author, February 27, 2017.

15. John Sedgwick, "Who the Devil Is Fred Rogers?," *Wigwag*, November 1989, 26, FRA.

16. Christopher de Vinck, interview by the author, March 15, 2018.

17. Melanie Chadwick Stevens, "Mr. Rogers' Neighborhood," *Parents Magazine*, May 1982, 78, FRA.

18. Mike Yaconelli, ed., "Mr. Fred Rogers," in *The Door Interviews* (Grand Rapids: Zondervan, 1989).

19. Fred Rogers, interview by Terry Gross, *Fresh Air* (radio), April 16, 1985, https://www.npr.org/templates/story/story.php?storyId=1178498.

20. "Gabby Hayes, Actor, Dies at 83; Comic in 200 Western Pic-

tures; Hopalong Cassidy's Pardner Was Best-Known Role – His First Career on Stage," *New York Times*, February 10, 1969.

21. Rogers, Television Academy Foundation interview.

22. Rogers, Television Academy Foundation interview.

23. King, *The Good Neighbor*, 90.

24. Rogers, Television Academy Foundation interview.

6. Whimsy and Seriousness on *The Children's Corner*

"Won't You Be My Neighbor?," words and music by Fred M. Rogers, 1967, © The McFeeley-Rogers Foundation.

1. Fred Rogers, in *Won't You Be My Neighbor?*, directed by Morgan Neville (Los Angeles: Universal Studios Home Entertainment, 2018), DVD.

2. Margaret Mary Kimmel and Mark Collins, "The Wonder of It All: Fred Rogers and the Story of an Icon" (Fred Rogers Center, September 2008), 10, FRA.

3. Fred Rogers, interview by Karen Herman, Television Academy Foundation, July 22, 1999, https://interviews.televisionacademy.com/interviews/fred-rogers.

4. Rogers, Television Academy Foundation interview.

5. Josie Carey, interview by Karen Herman, Television Academy Foundation, July 23, 1999, https://interviews.televisionacademy.com/interviews/josie-carey.

6. Rogers, Television Academy Foundation interview.

7. Carey, Television Academy Foundation interview.

8. Carey, Television Academy Foundation interview.

9. Carey, Television Academy Foundation interview.

10. Carey, Television Academy Foundation interview.

11. Rogers, Television Academy Foundation interview.

12. Carey, Television Academy Foundation interview.

13. Rogers, Television Academy Foundation interview.

14. "Je suis un tigre apprivoisé," Fred M. Rogers, 1954, © The McFeely-Rogers Foundation.

15. Carey, Television Academy Foundation interview.

16. Fred earned his bachelor of divinity degree in 1962. At the time, the bachelor of divinity was standard in the Presbyterian Church (UPCUSA) as well as in other denominations. As higher education stan-

dards evolved, the master of divinity degree became standard. As a result, in 1972, Pittsburgh Theological Seminary changed all prior bachelor of divinity degree titles to master of divinity.

17. Fred Rogers, letter to Fred B. Rainsberry, November 25, 1960, FRA.

18. Kimmel and Collins, "The Wonder of It All," 11.

19. Carey, Television Academy Foundation interview.

20. Carey, Television Academy Foundation interview.

21. Fred Rogers, letter to Fred B. Rainsberry, February 2, 1961, FRA.

22. Fred Rogers, "The Minister and the Young Child" (paper, Western Theological Seminary, December 1959), FRA. Rogers is quoting from Francis Thompson, "Shelley: An Essay," which originally appeared in the *Dublin Review* in July 1908, following Thompson's death. Thompson, in this excerpt, is quoting William Blake's poem "Auguries of Innocence."

23. Fred Rogers, "Re: a STORY," email message to Tom Junod, April 4, 1999, FRA.

7. Graduate Studies and Life-Transforming Teachers

"Did You Know?," words and music by Fred M. Rogers, 1979, © The McFeeley-Rogers Foundation.

1. "Fred Rogers – Ordained Evangelist Enters Field of Television Ministry," *Third Presbyterian Church Spire*, June 1963, 1, FRA.

2. Fred Rogers, "Invisible to the Eye" (speech, Pittsburgh Theological Seminary, May 24, 1994), 1, FRA. This document is a marked-up draft, partially typed, partially handwritten.

3. Fred Rogers, interview by Karen Herman, Television Academy Foundation, July 22, 1999, https://interviews.televisionacademy.com /interviews/fred-rogers.

4. Rogers, "Invisible to the Eye," 1.

5. Fred Rogers, "Dr. Orr Memorial Service Eulogy and Prayer" (September 27, 1993), 2, FRA.

6. Rogers, "Dr. Orr Memorial Service Eulogy," 4.

7. Rogers, "Invisible to the Eye," 15.

8. Rogers, "Invisible to the Eye," 15.

9. Mary Manz Simon, "Why Mister Rogers Tells Your Kids 'You Are Special': A Conversation with Fred Rogers," *Christian Parenting Today*, August 1994, 26, FRA.

10. Rogers, "Dr. Orr Memorial Service Eulogy," 2.

11. Rogers, "Invisible to the Eye," 16.

12. Rogers, "Dr. Orr Memorial Service Eulogy," 2–3.

13. Rogers, Television Academy Foundation interview.

14. Sally Ann Flecker, "When Fred Met Margaret: Mister Rogers' Mentor," *PittMed*, Winter 2018/2019, https://www.pittmed.health.pitt .edu/story/when-fred-met-margaret.

15. Rogers, Television Academy Foundation interview.

8. Canada, Fatherhood, and Separation

"I Like to Be Told," words and music by Fred M. Rogers, 1968, © The McFeeley-Rogers Foundation.

1. Maxwell King, *The Good Neighbor* (New York: Harry N. Abrams, 2018), 143.

2. King, *The Good Neighbor*, 150.

3. Fred Rogers, interview by Karen Herman, Television Academy Foundation, July 22, 1999, https://interviews.televisionacademy.com /interviews/fred-rogers.

4. From 1968 to 1970, the show's title was spelled *Misterogers' Neighborhood*, following the branding established by the CBC. Out of concern for children's learning to read, however, Rogers changed the title to *Mister Rogers' Neighborhood* starting with episode 1131, which aired February 15, 1971. Throughout this book, the American show's title has been standardized to the updated rendering.

5. Fred Rogers, speech for migrant workers, April 27, 1987, FRA, quoted in Michael G. Long, *Peaceful Neighbor: Discovering the Countercultural Mister Rogers* (Louisville: Westminster John Knox, 2015), 64.

6. Long, *Peaceful Neighbor*, 64.

7. Fred Rogers, "Speech for Association of Family and Conciliation Courts" (May 15, 1991), 6, FRA. Fred Rogers does not name Johnny in this speech but instead refers to him as a young man he knows. However, it is clear from the context and the age he cites that he is referring to Johnny.

8. Rogers, "Speech for Association of Family and Conciliation Courts."

9. King, *The Good Neighbor*, 150.

10. See Rogers, "Speech for Association of Family and Conciliation Courts."

11. Fred Rogers, letter to Senator H. J. Heinz III, January 31, 1991, FRA, quoted in Long, *Peaceful Neighbor*, 65.

9. Television and the Church

"The People You Like the Most," words and music by Fred M. Rogers, 1972, © The McFeeley-Rogers Foundation.

1. Margaret Mary Kimmel and Mark Collins, "The Wonder of It All: Fred Rogers and the Story of an Icon" (Fred Rogers Center, September 2008), 13, FRA.

2. Fred Rogers, in an interview by Tom Junod, in Tom Junod, "Can You Say . . . Hero?," *Esquire*, November 1998 (republished April 6, 2017), https://www.esquire.com/features/can-you-say-hero-esq1198.

3. Fred Rogers, "Prologue: At Play in the Neighborhood," in *Shakespeare Plays the Classroom*, ed. Stuart E. Omans and Maurice J. O'Sullivan (New York: Rowman & Littlefield, 2003, 2015).

4. Maxwell King, *The Good Neighbor: The Life and Work of Fred Rogers* (New York: Harry N. Abrams, 2018), 156–59.

5. Fred Rogers, "Children's TV: What Can the Church Do about It?," 1967, 1–3, FRA.

6. Rogers, "Children's TV," 1–2.

7. Rogers, "Children's TV," 2–4.

8. Eva Stimson, "The Real 'Mister Rogers': This Presbyterian Minister Is as Nice in Person as He Is on TV," *Adventist Review*, April 2000, http://archives.adventistreview.org/2003-1509/story5.html.

9. "Sunday on the Children's Corner, 1960," Pearl Digital Collections, Presbyterian Historical Society, accessed October 24, 2018, https://digital.history.pcusa.org/islandora/object/islandora:115991.

10. "Sunday on the Children's Corner, Revisited," Presbyterian Historical Society blog, February 15, 2018, https://www.history.pcusa.org/blog/2018/02/sunday-childrens-corner-revisited.

11. Music and lyrics by Josie Carey and Fred M. Rogers, © The McFeely-Rogers Foundation.

12. Fred Rogers, interview by Terry Gross, *Fresh Air* (radio), April 16, 1985, https://www.npr.org/templates/story/story.php?storyId=1178498.

13. Fred Rogers, interview by Karen Herman, Television Academy Foundation, July 22, 1999, https://interviews.televisionacademy.com/interviews/fred-rogers.

14. Wendy Murray Zoba, "Won't You Be My Neighbor? At the Center of Mister Rogers's Cheery Songs and Smiles Lies a God-Ordained Mission to Children," *Christianity Today*, March 6, 2000, https://www.christianitytoday.com/ct/2000/march6/1.38.html.

15. Felicity Barringer, "Mister Rogers Goes to Russia," *New York Times*, September 21, 1987, quoted in Michael G. Long, *Peaceful Neighbor: Discovering the Countercultural Mister Rogers* (Louisville: Westminster John Knox, 2015), 22.

16. Rogers, "Prologue."

10. Change, Fear, and Peace

"Peace and Quiet," words and music by Fred M. Rogers, 1968, © The McFeeley-Rogers Foundation.

1. Michael G. Long, *Peaceful Neighbor: Discovering the Countercultural Mister Rogers* (Louisville: Westminster John Knox, 2015), 3.

2. Long, *Peaceful Neighbor*, 3.

3. Long, *Peaceful Neighbor*, 9.

4. "Goodnight, God," words and music by Josie Carey and Fred M. Rogers, 1955, © The McFeely-Rogers Foundation.

11. Neighborhood Liturgy

"The Weekend Song," words and music by Fred M. Rogers, 1970, © The McFeeley-Rogers Foundation.

1. Maxwell King, *The Good Neighbor: The Life and Work of Fred Rogers* (New York: Harry N. Abrams, 2018), 75.

2. John Sedgwick, "Who the Devil Is Fred Rogers?," *Wigwag*, November 1989, 26, FRA.

3. Fred Rogers, *Dear Mister Rogers, Does It Ever Rain in Your Neighborhood? Letters to Mr. Rogers* (New York: Penguin, 1996), 40.

4. Sedgwick, "Who the Devil Is Fred Rogers?," 28.

5. Sam Newbury, memo to general managers and program managers, January 15, 1991, EU64, folder "EL daily, Jan. 1991," FRA, quoted in Michael G. Long, *Peaceful Neighbor: Discovering the Countercultural Mister Rogers* (Louisville: Westminster John Knox, 2015), 66.

6. Fred Rogers, interview by Karen Herman, Television Academy Foundation, July 22, 1999, https://interviews.televisionacademy.com/interviews/fred-rogers.

7. Sedgwick, "Who the Devil Is Fred Rogers?," 28.

8. *Mister Rogers' Neighborhood*, episode 1493, originally broadcast March 3, 1982, quoted in Long, *Peaceful Neighbor*, 165.

9. Eva Stimson, "The Real 'Mister Rogers': This Presbyterian Minister Is as Nice in Person as He Is on TV," *Adventist Review*, April 2000, http://archives.adventistreview.org/2003-1509/story5.html.

10. Tom Junod, "Can You Say . . . Hero?," *Esquire*, November 1998 (republished April 6, 2017), https://www.esquire.com/features/can-you-say-hero-esq1198.

11. Bill Isler, interview with the author, April 3, 2018.

12. Bill Isler, interview with the author.

13. Caroll Spinney, quoted in *It's You I Like*, directed by John Paulson (Arlington, VA: PBS Distribution, 2018), DVD.

14. Tim Madigan, *I'm Proud of You: My Friendship with Fred Rogers* (self-pub., CreateSpace, 2012), 154–55.

15. Sedgwick, "Who the Devil Is Fred Rogers?," 34.

12. Parables of the Kingdom

"Won't You Be My Neighbor?," words and music by Fred M. Rogers, 1967, © The McFeeley-Rogers Foundation.

1. Gladys Ford, "Creator of 'Mister Rogers' Neighborhood' Relates His Faith to TV Production," *Pittsburgh Presbyterian*, May–June 1985, 3, Mr. Rogers' Neighborhood Collection, 1955–2003, SC.1989.07, Archives & Special Collections, University of Pittsburgh Library System.

2. Fred Rogers, letter to Pauline Hubner, November 5, 1979, FRA, quoted in Michael G. Long, *Peaceful Neighbor: Discovering the Countercultural Mister Rogers* (Louisville: Westminster John Knox, 2015), xv.

3. Long, *Peaceful Neighbor*, 9–11.

4. "Peace and Quiet," Fred M. Rogers, 1968, © The McFeely-Rogers Foundation.

13. Difference in the Neighborhood

"I Like Someone Who Looks Like You," words and music by Fred M. Rogers, first appeared in 1992, © The McFeeley-Rogers Foundation.

1. For a thorough exploration of the treatment of difference in Mister Rogers' Neighborhood, see Long, *Peaceful Neighbor*.

2. "In the Neighborhood," episode 462 of *StoryCorps* (podcast), accessed December 19, 2018, https://storycorps.org/podcast/storycorps -462-in-the-neighborhood/.

3. "Remembering a Civil Rights Swim-In: 'It Was a Milestone,'" NPR, June 13, 2014, https://www.npr.org/2014/06/13/321380585/remem bering-a-civil-rights-swim-in-it-was-a-milestone.

4. Michael G. Long, *Peaceful Neighbor: Discovering the Countercultural Mister Rogers* (Louisville: Westminster John Knox, 2015), 87.

5. The observations in this paragraph are from Long, *Peaceful Neighbor*, 119–41 and 93.

6. Long, *Peaceful Neighbor*, 119–20.

7. Long, *Peaceful Neighbor*, 101–4.

8. Long, *Peaceful Neighbor*, 106, 140.

9. "It's You I Like," Fred M. Rogers, 1971, © The McFeely-Rogers Foundation.

10. Long, *Peaceful Neighbor*, 81–82.

11. Long, *Peaceful Neighbor*, 90.

12. The 1978 special "Christmas Eve on Sesame Street," for example, depicts David, played by African American actor Northern Calloway, and Maria, played by Puerto Rican American actor Sonia Manzano, as a couple. Their relationship is implied over several years, though Maria later marries Luis, another Latino/a character on the show.

13. Long, *Peaceful Neighbor*, 91.

14. "I'd Like to Be Just Like Mom and Dad," words and music by Fred M. Rogers, © The McFeely-Rogers Foundation.

15. Fred Rogers, interview by Karen Herman, Television Academy Foundation, July 22, 1999, https://interviews.televisionacademy.com /interviews/fred-rogers.

16. Mike Yaconelli, ed., "Mr. Fred Rogers," in *The Door Interviews* (Grand Rapids, MI: Zondervan, 1989).

17. See also Robert Bianco, "The Quiet Success of Fred Rogers," *Pittsburgh Press*, March 26, 1989, 12, Mr. Rogers' Neighborhood Collection,

1955–2003, SC.1989.07, Archives & Special Collections, University of Pittsburgh Library System, and Gladys Ford, "Creator of 'Mister Rogers' Neighborhood' Relates His Faith to TV Production," *Pittsburgh Presbyterian*, May–June 1985, 3, Mr. Rogers' Neighborhood Collection, 1955–2003, SC.1989.07, Archives & Special Collections, University of Pittsburgh Library System.

18. Long, *Peaceful Neighbor*, 112–13.

19. Michael Horton, interview with the author, March 15, 2018.

20. Fred Rogers, "Address" (speech, Thiel College, Greenville, Pennsylvania, November 13, 1969), 7, Mr. Rogers' Neighborhood Collection, 1955–2003, SC.1989.07, Archives & Special Collections, University of Pittsburgh Library System.

21. Christopher de Vinck, *The Power of the Powerless: A Brother's Legacy of Love* (New York: Doubleday, 1988; Crossroad, 2002), 149.

22. Tom Junod, "Can You Say . . . Hero?," *Esquire*, November 1998 (republished April 6, 2017), https://www.esquire.com/features/can-you-say-hero-esq1198.

23. Junod, "Can You Say . . . Hero?"

14. Puppets and Personality

"The Clown in Me," words and music by Fred M. Rogers, 1968, © The McFeeley-Rogers Foundation.

1. See Fred Rogers, "Invisible to the Eye" (speech, Pittsburgh Theological Seminary, May 24, 1994).

2. Mary Manz Simon, "Why Mister Rogers Tells Your Kids 'You Are Special': A Conversation with Fred Rogers," *Christian Parenting Today*, August 1994, 26, FRA.

3. Fred Rogers, interview by Karen Herman, Television Academy Foundation, July 22, 1999, https://interviews.televisionacademy.com/interviews/fred-rogers.

4. Robert Bianco, "The Quiet Success of Fred Rogers," *Pittsburgh Press*, March 26, 1989, 15–16, Mr. Rogers' Neighborhood Collection, 1955–2003, SC.1989.07, Archives & Special Collections, University of Pittsburgh Library System.

5. Fred Rogers, speech to the US Senate Subcommittee on Communications (under the Senate Commerce Committee), May 1, 1969. Video published online as "MISTER ROGERS' NEIGHBORHOOD | 1969

Senate Hearing | PBS KIDS," March 19, 2017, https://www.youtube.com /watch?v=J9uIJ-02yqQ&.

6. Tom Junod, "Can You Say . . . Hero?," *Esquire*, November 1998 (republished April 6, 2017), https://www.esquire.com/features/can-you -say-hero-esq1198.

7. John Sedgwick, "Who the Devil Is Fred Rogers?," *Wigwag*, November 1989, 32, FRA.

8. Sedgwick, "Who the Devil Is Fred Rogers?," 26.

9. Bianco, "The Quiet Success of Fred Rogers," 16.

10. Tom Junod, interview by the author, February 6, 2018.

11. Fred Rogers, Television Academy Foundation interview.

12. Sedgwick, "Who the Devil Is Fred Rogers?," 32.

13. John McCall, interview by the author, February 27, 2017.

14. "What Is Mister Rogers' Neighborhood?" (Family Communications, Inc., n.d.), Mr. Rogers' Neighborhood Collection, 1955–2003, SC.1989.07, Archives & Special Collections, University of Pittsburgh Library System.

15. "Sometimes I Wonder If I'm a Mistake," Fred M. Rogers, 1986, © The McFeely-Rogers Foundation.

16. Sedgwick, "Who the Devil Is Fred Rogers?," 34.

17. Kenneth A. Briggs, "Mr. Rogers Decides It's Time to Head for New Neighborhoods," *New York Times*, May 8, 1975, 45, https://www.ny times.com/1975/05/08/archives/mr-rogers-decides-its-time-to-head-for -new-neighborhoods.html.

18. Sedgwick, "Who the Devil Is Fred Rogers?," 28.

19. Nancy Greenberg, "A Beautiful Day: When You Visit Neighborhood of Mister Rogers," *The Sunday Bulletin*, February 16, 1975, 1, FRA.

20. Michael Horton, interview by the author, March 15, 2018.

21. Tim Madigan, interview by the author, March 19, 2018.

22. Madigan interview.

15. Friends and Neighbors

"Many Ways to Say I Love You," words and music by Fred M. Rogers, 1970, © The McFeeley-Rogers Foundation.

1. Bill Isler, interview by the author, April 3, 2018.

2. Tom Junod, interview by the author, February 6, 2018.

3. Junod interview.

4. Jim's mother was Fred's cousin, making Jim and Fred first cousins once removed.

5. Jim Okonak, interview by the author, March 6, 2017.

6. Michael Horton, interview by Maxwell King, in Maxwell King, *The Good Neighbor: The Life and Work of Fred Rogers* (New York: Harry N. Abrams, 2018), 200–201.

7. Betty Aberlin, letter to Fred Rogers, February 2, 1991, copy in private papers of Betty Aberlin, cited in Michael G. Long, *Peaceful Neighbor: Discovering the Countercultural Mister Rogers* (Louisville: Westminster John Knox, 2015), 69.

8. Amy Kaufman, "Fred Rogers' Family Keeps the Legacy of 'Mister Rogers' Neighborhood' Alive with a Candid New Documentary," *Los Angeles Times*, June 12, 2018, http://www.latimes.com/entertainment/movies/la-et-mn-mister-rogers-family-neighborhood-documentary-20180612-story.html.

9. François S. Clemmons, *A Song in My Soul: An Autobiographical Folktale*, unpublished book manuscript held in the private papers of François Clemmons, cited in Long, *Peaceful Neighbor*, 145.

10. Long, *Peaceful Neighbor*, 146.

11. Long, *Peaceful Neighbor*, 146.

12. Long, *Peaceful Neighbor*, 146.

13. Clemmons, *A Song in My Soul*.

14. Long, *Peaceful Neighbor*, 147.

15. François Clemmons, interview by the author, June 12, 2018.

16. Clemmons interview.

17. Michael Horton, interview by the author, March 15, 2018.

18. Michael Long, "'Wasn't He Gay?': A Revealing Question about Mister Rogers," *Huffington Post* (blog), October 22, 2014, https://www.huffingtonpost.com/michael-g-long/wasnt-he-gay-a-revealing-_b_6014538.html.

19. King, *The Good Neighbor*, 207.

20. Long, "'Wasn't He Gay?'"

21. John Sedgwick, "Who the Devil Is Fred Rogers?," *Wigwag*, November 1989, 29, FRA.

22. François Clemmons, in an interview from *Won't You Be My Neighbor?*, directed by Morgan Neville (Los Angeles: Universal Studios Home Entertainment, 2018), DVD.

23. William Hirsch, interview by Maxwell King, in King, *The Good Neighbor*, 208.

24. Fred Rogers, "Television and the Family" (speech, Symposium on the Family – Can it be saved?, Johnson & Johnson, April 26, 1975), 5, Mr. Rogers' Neighborhood Collection, 1955–2003, SC.1989.07, Archives & Special Collections, University of Pittsburgh Library System.

25. John McCall, interview by the author, February 27, 2017.

26. Letter to "Members and Friends of Sixth Church" from the Session of Sixth Presbyterian Church, Pittsburgh, Pennsylvania, April 2003, FRA.

27. Fred Rogers, letter to William G. Trudeau, September 23, 1975, FRA.

28. Fred Rogers, letter to Tom Junod, September 14, 1998, cited in Long, *Peaceful Neighbor*, 36.

29. Fred Rogers, "A Hero's Heroes," in "Fred Rogers: 1928–2003," *Pittsburgh Magazine*, April 2003, 55, FRA.

30. Jeanne Marie Laska, "Zen and the Art of Make Believe," *Pittsburgh Magazine*, October 1985, 45–46, Mr. Rogers' Neighborhood Collection, 1955–2003, SC.1989.07, Archives & Special Collections, University of Pittsburgh Library System.

31. "Everybody's Fancy," Fred M. Rogers, 1967, © The McFeeley-Rogers Foundation.

32. Hedda Sharapan, in an interview from *Won't You Be My Neighbor?*, directed by Morgan Neville (Los Angeles: Universal Studios Home Entertainment, 2018), DVD.

33. Long, "'Wasn't He Gay?'"

16. Fred's Big Feelings

"Sometimes People Are Good," words and music by Fred M. Rogers, 1967, © The McFeeley-Rogers Foundation.

1. Fred Rogers, "The Boundaries of Freedom" (sermon, Sixth Presbyterian Church, Pittsburgh, August 27, 1972), 2, FRA.

2. Rogers, "The Boundaries of Freedom," 3–4.

3. "The Truth Will Make Me Free," words and music by Fred M. Rogers, 1970, © The McFeely-Rogers Foundation.

4. Fred Rogers, speech to the US Senate Subcommittee on Communications (under Senate Commerce Committee), May 1, 1969. Video published online as "MISTER ROGERS' NEIGHBORHOOD | 1969 | Sen-

ate Hearing | PBS KIDS," March 19, 2017, https://www.youtube.com/watch?v=J9uIJ-02yqQ&.

5. "What Do You Do with the Mad that You Feel?," Fred M. Rogers, 1968, © The McFeely-Rogers Foundation.

6. Fred Rogers, *Dear Mister Rogers, Does It Ever Rain in Your Neighborhood? Letters to Mr. Rogers* (New York: Penguin, 1996), 18–19.

7. Fred Rogers, *Mister Rogers Talks with Families about Divorce* (n.p.: Hal Leonard Corporation, 1994), 38.

8. Rogers, *Mister Rogers Talks with Families about Divorce*, 92.

9. Mary Steigerwald, "The Ministry of Fred Rogers," *Mothering*, Spring 1984, 41, FRA.

10. Fred Rogers, "*Protestant Hour* Broadcast Script" (radio, February 25, 1976), 2–3, FRA.

11. Rogers, "*Protestant Hour* Broadcast Script," 2.

12. Michael Horton, interview by the author, March 15, 2018.

13. Tim Madigan, interview by the author, March 19, 2018.

14. Amy Hollingsworth, *The Simple Faith of Mister Rogers* (Nashville: Thomas Nelson, 2007), 135.

15. Amy Kaufman, "Fred Rogers' Family Keeps the Legacy of 'Mister Rogers' Neighborhood' Alive with a Candid New Documentary," *Los Angeles Times*, June 12, 2018, http://www.latimes.com/entertainment/movies/la-et-mn-mister-rogers-family-neighborhood-documentary-20180612-story.html.

16. Fred Rogers, "Dr. Orr Memorial Service Eulogy and Prayer" (September 27, 1993), 6, FRA.

17. "Fred Rogers: 1928–2003," *Pittsburgh Magazine*, April 2003, 57, FRA.

18. Fred Rogers, untitled notes, n.d., FRA.

19. Bill Isler, interview by the author, March 22, 2017.

20. Melanie Chadwick Stevens, "Mr. Rogers' Neighborhood," *Parents Magazine*, May 1982, 80, FRA.

21. Quoted in Maxwell King, *The Good Neighbor: The Life and Work of Fred Rogers* (New York: Harry N. Abrams, 2018), 315–16.

22. Fred Rogers, "More Than We Know" (address, Opening Ceremonies of the Sesquicentennial of Saint Vincent, Saint Vincent Archabbey Basilica, Latrobe, PA, April 25, 1995), 5–6, FRA.

17. All Ground as Holy Ground

"Goodnight, God," words and music by Josie Carey and Fred M. Rogers, 1955, © The McFeeley-Rogers Foundation.

1. Fred Rogers, "More Than We Know" (address, Opening Ceremonies of the Sesquicentennial of Saint Vincent, Saint Vincent Archabbey Basilica, Latrobe, PA, April 25, 1995), FRA.

2. Jim Okonak, interview by the author, March 6, 2017.

3. Service bulletin, "Ordination to the Ministry," Third Presbyterian Church, June 9, 1963, FRA.

4. Mary Manz Simon, "Why Mister Rogers Tells Your Kids 'You Are Special': A Conversation with Fred Rogers," *Christian Parenting Today*, August 1994, 26–27, FRA.

5. John McCall, interview by the author, February 27, 2017.

6. Eva Stimson, "The Real 'Mister Rogers': This Presbyterian Minister Is as Nice in Person as He Is on TV," *Adventist Review*, April 2000, http://archives.adventistreview.org/2003-1509/story5.html.

7. Wendy Murray Zoba, "Won't You Be My Neighbor? At the Center of Mister Rogers's Cheery Songs and Smiles Lies a God-Ordained Mission to Children," *Christianity Today*, March 6, 2000, https://www.christianitytoday.com/ct/2000/march6/1.38.html.

8. Stimson, "The Real 'Mister Rogers.'"

9. Mary Steigerwald, "The Ministry of Fred Rogers," *Mothering*, Spring 1984, 41, FRA.

10. Iris Krasnow, "Mr. Rogers Distributes Blessed Self-Assurance," *Washington Times Magazine*, June 18, 1985, Mr. Rogers' Neighborhood Collection, 1955–2003, SC.1989.07, Archives & Special Collections, University of Pittsburgh Library System.

11. Betsy Weaver, "Mr. Rogers: There's No Movie Star Here," *Boston Parents Paper*, July 1986, 8, FRA.

12. Fred Rogers, "Invisible to the Eye" (speech, Pittsburgh Theological Seminary, May 24, 1994), FRA.

13. Jonathan Merritt, "Saint Fred," *Atlantic*, November 22, 2015, https://www.theatlantic.com/politics/archive/2015/11/mister-rogers-saint/416838/.

14. Fred Rogers, interview by Karen Herman, Television Academy Foundation, July 22, 1999, https://interviews.televisionacademy.com/interviews/fred-rogers.

15. Krasnow, "Mr. Rogers Distributes Blessed Self-Assurance."

16. Chris Buczinsky, "The Performance of the Pastoral," in *Revisiting Mister Rogers' Neighborhood: Essays on Lessons about Self and Community*, ed. Kathy Merlock Jackson and Steven M. Emmanuel (Jefferson, NC: McFarland, 2016), 10.

17. Fred Rogers, "Invisible to the Eye" (speech, Johnson & Johnson, December 8, 1994), 7, FRA.

18. John Sedgwick, "Who the Devil Is Fred Rogers?," *Wigwag*, November 1989, 29, FRA.

19. Tom Junod, "Great Minds . . . ," email message to Fred Rogers, February 22, 1999.

20. Fred Rogers, "Re: Great Minds . . . ," email message to Tom Junod, February 22, 1999.

21. Krasnow, "Mr. Rogers Distributes Blessed Self-Assurance."

22. Fred Rogers, "Latrobe High School Baccalaureate Speech" (Latrobe, PA, June 2, 1996), FRA.

23. Rogers, "Latrobe High School Baccalaureate Speech."

24. "Mr. Rogers Was a Friend to Everyone. But to One Sick Little Girl, He Was a Life Saver," WKYC, December 6, 2018, https://www.wkyc.com/article/syndication/heartthreads/mr-rogers-was-a-friend-to-everyone-but-to-one-sick-little-girl-he-was-a-life-saver/507-621514588.

25. François Clemmons, interview by the author, March 22, 2017.

26. Rev. Lisa B. Hamilton, interview by the author, April 8, 2018.

27. Lisa Belcher-Hamilton, "The Gospel According to Fred: A Visit with Mr. Rogers," *Christian Century*, April 13, 1994.

28. Steigerwald, "The Ministry of Fred Rogers," 41.

29. Rogers, Television Academy Foundation interview.

18. Heaven Is a Neighborhood

"Goodnight, God," words and music by Josie Carey and Fred M. Rogers, 1955, © The McFeeley-Rogers Foundation.

1. "Episode 1765," The Mister Rogers' Neighborhood Archive (website), accessed December 31, 2018, http://www.neighborhoodarchive.com/mrn/episodes/1765/index.html.

2. Joanne Rogers, in an interview from *Won't You Be My Neighbor?*, directed by Morgan Neville (Los Angeles: Universal Studios Home Entertainment, 2018), DVD.

3. Tim Madigan, "From Mister Rogers: Words of Wisdom as Warm as His Sweater," *Cape Cod Times*, December 21, 2003, FRA.

4. Maxwell King, *The Good Neighbor: The Life and Work of Fred Rogers* (New York: Harry N. Abrams, 2018), 345–46.

5. King, *The Good Neighbor*, 346.

6. King, *The Good Neighbor*, 347.

7. King, *The Good Neighbor*, 348.

8. Yo-Yo Ma, in an interview from *Won't You Be My Neighbor?* (documentary).

9. Madigan, "From Mister Rogers."

10. Barbara Vancheri, "As promised, Joanne Rogers is doing 'fine,'" *Pittsburgh Post-Gazette*, December 25, 2003, http://old.post-gazette.com /localnews/20031225closeup1225p3.asp.

11. Fred Rogers, letter to Janet Harris, January 28, 1978, CW10, folder "Rogers, Fred, Daily—January 1979," FRA, quoted in Michael G. Long, *Peaceful Neighbor: Discovering the Countercultural Mister Rogers* (Louisville: Westminster John Knox, 2015), 32.

12. Wendy Murray Zoba, "Won't You Be My Neighbor? At the Center of Mister Rogers's Cheery Songs and Smiles Lies a God-Ordained Mission to Children," *Christianity Today*, March 6, 2000, https://www .christianitytoday.com/ct/2000/march6/1.38.html.

13. John Sedgwick, "Who the Devil Is Fred Rogers?," *Wigwag*, November 1989, 27–28, FRA.

14. Jeanne Marie Laskas, "Zen and the Art of Make Believe," *Pittsburgh Magazine*, October 1985, 48, Mr. Rogers' Neighborhood Collection, 1955–2003, SC.1989.07, Archives & Special Collections, University of Pittsburgh Library System.

15. Laskas, "Zen and the Art of Make Believe," 49.

16. Fred Rogers, "More Than We Know" (address, Opening Ceremonies of the Sesquicentennial of Saint Vincent, Saint Vincent Archabbey Basilica, Latrobe, PA, April 25, 1995), FRA.

17. Alan Borsuk, "Everyone's Neighbor," *Milwaukee Journal Sentinel*, May 20, 2001, quoted in Long, *Peaceful Neighbor*, 32.

18. Fred Rogers, "!!," email message to Tom Junod, May 29, 1999.

19. Rogers, Television Academy Foundation interview.

20. Joanne Rogers, in an interview from *Won't You Be My Neighbor?*, DVD.

21. Joanne Rogers, in an interview from *Won't You Be My Neighbor?*, DVD.

22. "Fred Rogers: 1928–2003," *Pittsburgh Magazine*, April 2003, 39, FRA.

23. "'A Gentle Soul': Fans, Colleagues and Celebrities React to a Personal Loss," *Pittsburgh Post-Gazette*, February 28, 2003, FRA.

24. Fred Rogers, "Invisible to the Eye" (speech, Pittsburgh Theological Seminary, May 24, 1994), 13, FRA.

25. "Fred Rogers: 1928–2003," 33.